Illinois Central College
Learning Resources Center

Economic Heresies

ECONOMIC HERESIES Some Old-Fashioned Questions in Economic Theory

JOAN ROBINSON, 1903-

BASIC BOOKS, INC., PUBLISHERS / NEW YORK

© 1971 by Basic Books, Inc.

Library of Congress Catalog Card Number: 71–147012

SBN 465–01786–X

Manufactured in the United States of America

PREFACE

While working on this book I have profited very much from arguments and discussions with a number of colleagues and pupils. I would like particularly to mention Professor A. Asimakopulos of McGill University, Mr. John Eatwell of Trinity College, Cambridge, Dr. Amit Bhaduri now at the Indian Institute of Statistics (Calcutta), and Mr. Jan Kregel of the University of Bristol.

A large part of Chapter 6, *Prices and Money,* appears as an article in the *Journal of Money, Credit and Banking,* November 1970, under the title "Quantity Theories Old and New."

Cambridge
December, 1970

INTRODUCTION

The orthodox doctrines of economics which were dominant in the last quarter of the nineteenth century had a clear message. They supported laisser faire, free trade, the gold standard, and the universally advantageous effects of the pursuit of profit by competitive private enterprise. This was acceptable to the authorities in an expanding and flourishing capitalist world, especially to the authorities in England,[1] which was still felt to be the dominant center and chief beneficiary of the system.

The arguments on which the economists' doctrines were based, however, had little relevance to the problems on which they pronounced. The structure of economic theory was a deductive system based on a priori premises, such as that the behavior of individuals is governed by the principle of maximizing utility; the argument was set up in terms of the effects of a displacement from an already established equilibrium or in terms of comparisons between two equilibrium positions, without any discussion of the process of changing from one to another. For instance, the case for free trade, which was a central part of orthodox teaching, was based upon comparing the situation of two countries, each in isolation in a stationary state, with given resources fully employed under the rules of perfect competition,

[1] This was true of England, rather than of Great Britain or the United Kingdom as a whole.

vii

viii / *Introduction*

with the situation in which they are trading in equilibrium, imports being equal to exports, with everything else unchanged. (Even then, the argument that neither country could improve its position by protection contained a logical flaw; this scandal was hushed up in academic teaching until it broke out again in the 1930s, when orthodox doctrine as well as the world economy was in a state of disarray.) [2] The lack of correspondence between the assumptions of theory and the facts in reality did not matter because the doctrines were acceptable; since the main doctrine was laisser faire, no prescriptions for any positive policy were required; there was no need to bother about studying situations to which policy might have to be applied. The economists could go on happily categorizing empty boxes without feeling any need to fill them with information.

After 1918, the situation of the British economy in the world was drastically changed but the economists had not believed themselves to be influenced by English national interests; their doctrines had always been set up as universal truths; they were now carried over into a situation where they were no longer appropriate. There was one fact which was particularly awkward. While the United States was enjoying the long boom of the 1920s, Great Britain was suffering from low profits and heavy unemployment. Now, it was an axiom of the orthodox scheme, inherited from the classics, that there cannot be unemployment because of Say's Law. When a program was suggested in 1929 for public expenditure to relieve unemployment, it was answered by the famous Treasury View,[3] according to which there is a fixed fund of saving available to finance investment. If the government borrows part to spend upon public works, there will be an exactly equal reduction in foreign investment, so that un-

2 See A. Lerner, "The Diagrammatical Representation of Demand Conditions in International Trade," *Economica* (August 1934).

3 See *Memoranda on Certain Proposals Relating to Unemployment*, Cmd. 3331.

employment due to the reduction of the balance of trade would more or less completely offset the increase in employment due to public works. Soon the world slump set in. The total bankruptcy of the orthodox theory became evident to all but its professional devotees and the Keynesian Revolution emerged from the ruins.

On the plane of the development of ideas, the main point of the General Theory was that it broke out of the theological system of orthodox axioms; Keynes was looking at the actual situation and trying to understand how an actual economy operates; he brought the argument down from timeless stationary states into the present, here and now, when the past cannot be changed and the future cannot be known.

At the time it seemed like a revolution; a new day had dawned in which economics was going to be a serious subject concerned with serious problems. But the day soon clouded over. After 1945, Keynes' innovations had become orthodox in their turn; now governments had to admit that they were concerned with maintaining the level of employment; but in respect to economic theory the old theology closed in again. Keynes himself began the reconstruction of the orthodox scheme that he had shattered. "But if our central controls succeed in establishing an aggregate volume of output corresponding to full employment as nearly as is practicable, the classical theory comes into its own again from this point onwards. . . . It is in determining the volume, not the direction of actual employment that the existing system has broken down." [4] He had been too much occupied with immediate problems to think very much about what the neoclassical theory (which he called classical) really entailed. In some moods he found capitalism morally and aesthetically abhorrent but his object was to save it from destroying itself; he did not

---

[4] John Maynard Keynes, *The General Theory of Employment, Interest and Money* (London: Macmillan, 1936), pp. 378–379.

press his criticism either of the system or of its apologists very deep. In particular he did not distinguish between profitable investment and socially beneficial investment, and he was rather averse to considering problems connected with the distribution of income between families in an industrial nation (the problem of distribution of income in the world had not yet come into fashion).

A new orthodoxy was soon established by a simple device. A substitute for Say's Law was provided by the assumption that a well-managed Keynesian policy keeps investment running at the level which absorbs the saving forthcoming at full employment. The rest of the doctrines of the neoclassics could then be revived.

The neo-neoclassics, however, seem to have overlooked some serious inconsistencies in the old scheme which made the new synthesis unsatisfactory.

For instance, there is an inconsistency between the assumption of a perfectly competitive market and the assumption that every trader is maximizing his gain. A group of individuals, say sellers of a particular commodity, can increase the gain for each other by acting in concert. This was the flaw in the case for free trade. Even within the strict assumptions of the argument, it could be shown that either country can gain an advantage from turning the terms of trade in its favor by restricting the supply of its product and reducing its demand for the product of the other. In the pursuit of self-interest, each country will try to gain at the expense of the rest of the world. Free trade is not an equilibrium position unless it is enforced by general agreement.[5]

Another drawback of the neoclassical scheme was that it was fully worked out only for a stationary state while the neo-neoclassics wanted to make use of it to discuss the now fashionable

---

[5] Cf. T. Scitovsky, "A Reconsideration of the Theory of Tariffs," *Review of Economic Studies* (Summer 1942).

concept of continuous growth. A hitherto stationary economy cannot begin to grow without going through a drastic transformation—for instance, its investment industries, which have been operating at a level just to keep their stock of equipment intact, must be expanded sufficiently to allow for net investment. Moreover, if the impulse to grow arises from a desire of individual households to save, how is the initial Keynesian slump to be overcome? Marshall wanted to discuss growth but he was daunted by the problem of adapting the formal theory to deal with it. "In fact we are here verging on the high theme of economic progress; and here therefore it is especially needful to remember that economic problems are imperfectly presented when they are treated as problems of statical equilibrium, and not of organic growth." [6] The neo-neoclassicals plunged in without any such hesitation.

The most serious problem concerned the concept of "factors of production." One view was expounded by Wicksteed: "We must regard every kind and quality of labour that can be distinguished from other kinds and qualities as a separate factor; and in the same way every kind of land will be taken as a separate factor. Still more important is it to insist that instead of speaking of so many £ worth of capital we shall speak of so many ploughs, so many tons of manure, and so many horses, or foot-pounds of 'power.' Each of these may be scheduled in its own unit, and when this has been done the enumeration of the factors of production may be regarded as complete." [7] This point of view underlies the Walrasian scheme.

From another point of view factors of production are treated

---

[6] A. Marshall, *Principles of Economics* (New York: Macmillan) p. 461. Except where otherwise stated, references to Marshall's *Principles* are to the eighth edition.

[7] P. H. Wicksteed, *An Essay on the Co-ordination of the Laws of Distribution* (London: Macmillan, 1894), p. 33. Reprinted in Scarce Tracts series, London School of Economics.

in the broad categories of Ricardo—land, labor, and capital. The nature of capital was always a source of anxiety and trouble. Marshall divided the factors of production into land, labor, and waiting, and he regarded the *real* cost of production (as opposed to rent of natural resources) as composed of the efforts of work and the sacrifice of waiting. Now, waiting consists of owning property and refraining from selling out and spending the proceeds. "That surplus benefit which a person gets in the long run by postponing enjoyment, and which is measured by the rate of interest (subject as we have seen to certain conditions), is the reward of *waiting*. He may have obtained the *de facto* possession of property by inheritance or by any other means, moral or immoral, legal or illegal. But if, having the power to consume that property in immediate gratifications, he chooses to put it in such a form as to afford him deferred gratifications, then any superiority there may be in deferred gratification over those immediate ones is the reward of his waiting. When he lends out the wealth on a secure loan the net payment which he receives for the use of the wealth may be regarded as affording a numerical measure of that reward." [8]

Thus the total stock of capital of an economy at any moment has two aspects: it is a great collection of various kinds of equipment, stocks, and work in progress, and it is a sum of wealth. There is a third aspect of capital which mediates between the other two, that is, capital as finance. An entrepreneur may own wealth or borrow from rentiers. The command of finance permits him to employ labor; wages are paid out week by week in advance of the production of salable goods; when the goods are sold (if all has gone according to plan) the initial finance is recovered with a profit. If the delay is, say, six months, a loan

---

[8] Marshall, *Principles*, 1st ed., 1890, p. 614. Here Marshall clearly regards *waiting* as simply owning capital. In later editions a similar passage is applied to waiting in the sense of saving (8th ed., 1920, p. 233), and the argument becomes extremely obscure.

equal to half one year's wage bill provides a wage fund which permits him to employ labor indefinitely, as long as the same conditions hold. He also advances raw materials, power, and other running costs which will be recovered from sales over the course of some months and he advances equipment, the finance of which is to be recovered over the course of some years. Thus finance is the link between capital as physical means of production and capital as wealth.

Real productivity from the point of view of society belongs to physical equipment and materials which embody technical know-how; profit belongs to capital as finance embodied in business organization, and interest (the reward of waiting) belongs to rentier wealth. Marshall was evidently conscious of the difficulty of identifying the reward of waiting with the productivity of physical capital goods; when capital comes into the analysis, the smoke screen of ambiguity which covers the whole argument of the *Principles* grows thicker than ever; but the neo-neoclassicals do not seem to have felt any difficulty about it. (A recent textbook, *The Neoclassical Theory of Production and Distribution* by Professor C. E. Ferguson, is valuable because the author, as he declares, has faith in the theory and is not afraid to make it clear and definite.[9] He sets out a number of propositions in which inputs consist of labor and physical capital goods of various kinds, following Walras; then he turns to the economy as a whole and treats capital as a whole as an input which can be treated in the same way as the input of, say, the services of a particular kind of machine. Wages are accounted for by the marginal product of labor, and profit by the marginal product of capital.)

Apart from logical incoherence, the flaw in the new orthodoxy destroys the validity of its message. The deepest layer in neo-

---

[9] C. E. Ferguson, *The Neoclassical Theory of Production and Distribution* (Cambridge: Cambridge University Press, 1969), see p. XVII.

classical thought was the conception of society as a harmonious whole, without internal conflicts of interest. Society, under the guidance of the hidden hand, allocates its resources between particular uses in such a way as to maximize utility; society decides the allocation of resources between present consumption and accumulation to permit greater consumption in the future. Accumulation is represented by Robinson Crusoe transferring some of his activity from gathering nuts to eat to making a fishing rod; or by the sturdy peasant who cuts timber in the forest to build himself a durable hut.[10] Here saving means a sacrifice of present consumption or leisure to increase productivity for the future; saving and investment are two aspects of the same behavior. Keynes destroyed this part of the analogy by showing that, in a private enterprise economy, investments are made by profit-seeking firms and it is they who decide for society how much it will save. But he let the rest of the analogy stand. He was immediately concerned with a situation where investment, on any criterion, was manifestly too low; he maintained that, while beneficial investments were to be preferred, *any* investment was better than none. But once Keynes has become orthodox, the case is altered. If we are to be guaranteed near-full employment the question comes up, what form should employment take? The neo-neoclassicals have dodged that question. Adopting the slogan that the rate of return on investment to an individual firm measures, corresponds to, or is derived from, the marginal product of capital to society, they have reconstructed the case for laisser faire.

The new doctrine is now coming to a crisis. The first part of the doctrine—that the amount of investment is controlled by how much society wants to save—was discredited in the great slump. The second part, that the form of investment is controlled by the principle of maximizing the welfare of society,

---

10 Cf. Marshall, *Principles,* p. 351.

is being discredited by the awakening of public opinion to the persistence of poverty—even hunger—in the wealthiest nations, the decay of cities, the pollution of environment, the manipulation of demand by salesmanship, the vested interests in war, not to mention the still more shocking problems of the world outside the prosperous industrial economies. The complacency of neo-laisser faire cuts the economists off from discussing the economic problems of today just as Say's Law cut them off from discussing unemployment in the world slump.

It seems that this second crisis, like the first, is due to the uncritical acceptance of the apologetic that seemed plausible (though it was never logical) in the late nineteenth century. In these essays I attempt to find the roots of modern orthodoxy in the neoclassical tradition.

It seems that modern orthodoxy is mainly based upon Walras, which narrows its scope. The tradition of Marshall, though full of confusions and sophistries, was much richer. Many of the problems that we used to discuss in the 1930s have been lost from the canon. I hope that a reexamination of the old-fashioned questions will help to clear the way for a more penetrating discussion of the problems of today.

CONTENTS

Economic Heresies

1

STATIONARY
STATES

To find a stationary economy in real life we should look for some corner of the world untouched by war and trade where tradition rules and the cycle of production and distribution repeats itself from year to year, from generation to generation, without changes in population, technical innovations, or concentration of wealth. But, in such a society, prices, incomes, and property are also ruled by tradition. Analogies with modern capitalism may be found in it, but they will be too farfetched to be convincing. The stationary state in economic theory was not supposed to describe any actual society. It was an analytical device intended to throw light upon relationships in the changing world in which the economists were living.

For Adam Smith, Ricardo, and Marx the central subject of discussion was the accumulation of means of production and of property. In a stationary state there is no accumulation. The neoclassical school, which came into fashion in the second half of the nineteenth century, introduced two quite distinct ways of eliminating accumulation from models which were intended in other respects to correspond to reality. One was to consider the situation, so to speak, today, with the physical stocks of commodities and means of production that happen to be in existence;

3

the other was to consider the situation at Kingdom Come when the process of accumulation has been completed and no one finds it worthwhile to acquire anything more. These two opposite kinds of stationary states are unfortunately often confused in modern textbooks.[1]

WALRAS

The first kind is the basis of Walras' market where the relative prices of commodities are determined by supply and demand. Walras (and his modern disciples) tells us more about the commodities than about the people concerned. Each trader enters the market with something to offer. Is he a specialist? If so, his command of purchasing power depends very much upon the price that his particular commodity commands in terms of other things. He may do very well out of the market or he may come away with less than will feed his family till the next meeting. This aspect of the matter is very little discussed. To ensure that there must be an equilibrium pattern of prices reconciling the supply of arbitrarily given stocks of various kinds of commodities with the demand, which is governed by whatever happens to be the tastes and desires of the traders, it is necessary to allow for the possibility of a zero price for a commodity for which supply exceeds demand at any positive price. If some of the traders have nothing else to offer except such a commodity, what is to become of them?

There is one case that has been observed in real life which corresponds pretty well to the Walrasian conception of equilibrium between supply and demand arrived at by a process of "groping" through bids and offers by traders. This is in a prisoner-of-war camp.[2] The men are kept alive more or less by

---

[1] Cf. above, p. xiii.
[2] See R. A. Radford, "The Economic Organization of a P.O.W. Camp," *Economica* (November 1945).

official rations and they receive parcels from the Red Cross once a month. The contents of the parcels are not tailored to the tastes of the individual recipients, so that it is possible for each to gain by swapping what he wants less for what he wants more. A market is formed when the parcels are opened and prices, offered and bid, are quoted in terms of cigarettes. Trading and retrading take place until demand is equated to supply for each commodity (there are not likely to be any zero prices in such a situation!) and each trader, at the prices ruling, has no further desire to exchange one thing for another.[3] Each trader has an initial endowment (his parcel) more or less the same as every other and each comes away with a roughly equal value of consumables. The problem of the distribution of consumption being governed by prices is therefore not very important.

Anyone who happened to prefer just what was in his parcel need not trade. Each swaps only to get something that he likes better than what he has. Thus trade makes everyone subjectively better off. (This is a good advertisement for trade which does not apply to specialist producers, say, of cocoa beans or rubber, who may find one day that the laws of supply and demand have reduced them to misery.)

In the prison-camp market, cigarettes are used as a unit of account and, perhaps, as a medium of exchange in three-cornered transactions, but there is no store of value, no "link between the present and the future." [4] All commodities are consumed within the month and a fresh set of prices is established when a fresh lot of parcels arrive. In this sense it is a nonmonetary economy. Though prices are quoted in a single unit, the value of an ounce of each commodity really consists in its potential purchasing power over all other commodities. The overall price level in terms of cigarettes is no more significant than the

---

[3] No doubt a sense of what is proper behavior rules out the formation of monopolies; cf. above, p. viii.

[4] See Keynes, *General Theory,* p. 293.

price level in terms of pounds of cheese, or of anything else.

The whole point of this case is that the parcels are simply given. Each item has its opportunity cost in terms of other things that it might be exchanged for but there are no costs of production and no choice of what to produce. To extend the notion of a nonmonetary stationary state to an economy with production going on is not so easy. We have to assume that there are given stocks, not of consumable commodities, but of "factors of production." There is a given labor force, an area of land with particular types of soil in particular locations, a certain amount of productive equipment, such as buildings, roads, and machines of various kinds, and stocks of raw materials. The equipment and stocks were produced in the past but the amount of each kind in existence "today" is quite arbitrary. The raw materials are used up and reproduced week by week and the equipment is kept intact in the process of production, like well-farmed land.

Workers offer their services for wages and owners of land, machines, and so forth, offer the services of means of production for a hire-price or rent. (It is misleading, as we shall see in a moment, to call machines "capital" and their rent "profit.") Recipients of income buy commodities produced by the factors, according to their needs and tastes and according to the purchasing power that each commands. There is no separate source of income from organizing production. (Managers are a type of worker.) Workers may hire machines or owners of machines hire workers, or there may be a disembodied spirit, an auctioneer, who registers all bids and offers. Prices are quoted in terms of some unit of account. At intermediate stages in the bargaining process there may be an excess or a deficiency of demand for a particular commodity. Its price is then raised or lowered, and its output increased or reduced, as the case may be. The stock of equipment cannot be altered but insofar as particular machines are versatile they can be directed to one use or another according to which offers the best rent.

This argument is very hard to grasp, for a process which would take a long (perhaps indefinite) time to work out is conceived to be instantaneous. But the story is not meant to be taken literally. The only point of it is to argue that there is a set of prices, wages, and rents that provides an equilibrium position.

In equilibrium, the supply and demand for each commodity are equal. This means that, with the ruling prices and his own income, no individual wants to buy more of one thing or less of another than he is doing. Similarly, with the ruling prices at which commodities can be sold and the ruling levels of wages and rents, no producer would find some other combination of factors profitable. The price of a pound, or yard, or pint of any commodity is just sufficient to cover its average share of the cost of wages for particular types of labor, replacement of raw materials, and rents for the particular pieces of equipment that are producing the flow of output in which it forms part.

If the supply of any particular machine is in excess of demand its rent is zero. Similarly, if labor were in excess of demand, wages would be zero. This is clearly incompatible with equilibrium, for the labor force could not be kept in being with nothing to eat. To get out of this difficulty it is assumed that technical conditions are such that there is substitutability between factors of production, in the sense that the output of a commodity can always be increased by using a larger physical amount of one factor with a fixed amount of the others. When the use of one factor alone is increased, the proportional increment of product is less than the proportional increment of the factor; there are diminishing returns between factors or falling marginal productivity of the increasing factor as the physical proportions of factors change. The operation of the auctioneer ensures that, in equilibrium, no factors are employed in a combination where one enjoys increasing returns; if it did, the return on employing it would be greater than its hire-price and more would be used.

In equilibrium the factors are used in such proportions, in the production of each commodity, that the value of the marginal product of each (in terms of the unit of account) is not less than its hire-price per physical unit. Thus if, at a certain stage in the bargaining process, some labor were unemployed, the wage would be reduced and it would become profitable to employ more labor with the given physical amount of other factors. This is plausible enough when the other factor is land. Agricultural technique can be adapted to a wide range of intensity of cultivation. Machines are not so versatile, but the adaptation may be supposed to be made, up to a certain limit, by shift working or there may be better and worse designs among the arbitrarily given stock of machines so that a lower wage rate makes machines with a lower output per man-hour worth using. In that case, in equilibrium (provided that the total stock of machines is more than enough to provide full employment at a subsistance wage) the least productive machine in use in some or all lines may have zero rent, like Ricardo's marginal land.

In this model a low wage rate does not create a problem of effective demand. The lower the wages, the higher the rents. Workers consume less and property owners more.

Each piece of land and each machine receives its appropriate rent, depending on its technical productivity, the availability of other factors, and the demand for its product. There is no general rate of profit on the value of capital or expected rate of return on new investment. If we introduced into the picture a rate of interest—a price for purchasing power today to be repaid (or reborrowed) at a future date—the equilibrium of the system would be upset.

Interest may be regarded as a hire-price for finance but it is quite unlike the wages and rents of factors of production. It is expressed as value per unit of value while they are expressed as value per unit of a physical service—a man-hour of labor of a particular type or the use for a year of a particular machine.

With a standard rate of interest in the market, each machine and each acre would have a capital value such that its rent divided by that value was equal to the rate of interest. These values would bear no regular relation to the past cost or present reproduction cost of machines. It would then be profitable to produce those for which value exceeded cost. Expectations of change, investment, and saving have to be brought into the story and the auctioneer has to be conceived to be capable of registering bids and offers spread over an indefinite future. Moreover, there has to be some story to account for how the rate of interest is determined.

KINGDOM COME

A story is provided in the model of the other kind of stationary state, though not a very plausible one. There, the rate of interest is determined by the tastes and habits of the owners of property. They require a certain return on their wealth—the "reward of waiting"—in order to prevent them from consuming it in "present gratifications." [5] They get this return by lending finance to entrepreneurs who use it to acquire and operate means of production which earn profits. So long as the rate of interest—the hire-price of finance—is less than the rate of return to be confidently expected on investment, the stock of capital goods is accumulating. The stationary state is reached when the two are equal.

For the sake of a convenient label, we may call this model Pigovian, for it was Pigou who drew out the concept of a stationary state from the others that it is mingled with in Marshall's *Principles.* In the Pigovian model the stock of equipment is not just arbitrarily given "today." The rate of interest is a supply

---

[5] See above, p. xii.

price for capital. In stationary equilibrium, the value of the stock of capital goods in existence is such that the value of the annual net profit covers this supply price.

This model, though not particularly convincing, is much less difficult to grasp than the first one. We are not confined to a thin slice of time "today." No change is occurring but time rolls on from the past into the future. The stock of equipment and the amount of wealth are constant because the owners and operators choose that they should be. No one is saving or making net investment because no one wants to do so. Production is organized, not by a ghostly auctioneer but in business firms which operate plants and employ labor. Equipment is being kept intact, not because it happens to exist, but because the firms decide to keep it intact. (We can now admit amortization of capital as an element in cost of production, which is difficult to accommodate in the first model.) However, since there are perfectly confident expectations that the future will be exactly like the past, there is no more scope for "enterprise" than in the Walrasian model. The firms must be supposed to pay their managers and earn just enough gross profit to keep the value of their capital intact and to pay the standard rate of interest on it.

We can now leave the bewildering calculation of relative values and introduce a price level in terms of money. The wage rate, the hire-price of labor, is fixed in terms of a unit of money. (There may be different rates for different levels of skill, etc., but the composition of the labor force has become adjusted to the pattern of demand, just like the stocks of equipment.)

Now, with given money-wage rates, a given corpus of technical knowledge, and a uniform rate of profit on capital, there is a determinate set of money prices for all commodities and means of production. (It is possible to borrow from the other model an arbitrarily fixed supply of "land" but it is more congenial to this model to suppose that all means of production are reproducible.) Technical conditions specify the input-output table for the whole economy in terms of labor and means of production, each in its own physical unit. The requirement of a uniform rate of profit settles relative prices, including the wage rate in terms of any commodity, and the money-wage rate settles money prices. (If money as a medium of exchange is in use, the quantity of it in existence is just what is required to pay wages and carry out transactions at the ruling prices.) [6]

The flow of money incomes—wages and interest—is purchasing the flow of output of consumption goods; the composition of output is such that the consumers are willing to buy what is offered at the ruling prices. The stock of equipment is appropriate to producing this output while keeping itself intact. There may be other techniques known but those that have been chosen are those which (at the ruling prices and wage rates) make it possible to earn a profit equal to the ruling rate of interest on finance invested. None can earn more and any that earned less would not have been installed.

The price of each product is such that it can pay the wage for all the labor required to produce it directly, and indirectly through the replacement of stocks of materials and wear and tear of plant, while paying the rate of profit on the value of all the capital directly and indirectly required to produce it.

The cost of labor in terms of his own product to each employer is such that the excess of the value of output over the wage bill pays all other costs. Thus the cost of labor in terms of product is less the greater the value of capital per man employed. The real wage in the cost-of-living sense depends upon the level of prices of those commodities which workers want to buy. Given the rate of profit, the level of real wages in both senses depends upon the technology in use.

---

[6] Since the rate of interest has to be equal to the "reward of waiting" there is no scope for introducing a rate of interest based on the demand and supply of money.

The microequilibrium of the system depends upon the rule that competition is obliging the firms to produce a given output at minimum cost. To each individually, the wage rate, the rate of interest, and all prices are given independently of his own behavior; he combines the factors of production in such a way that the marginal *net* product of each is not less than its supply price. That is, in considering how much of each factor to employ, the cost of other factors and the selling price of the product are taken into account. (This is a different concept from the marginal physical product of the Walrasian model; Marshall set the fashion for confusing them in his famous footnote about the marginal shepherd,[7] by cooking the example so as to make them identical.)

But now we come to a serious snag. There is nothing in the model to show that the available labor force is being employed. The owners of property have as much as they are willing to own at the ruling rate of interest and the firms are operating as much plant as will yield the corresponding rate of profit when the wage bill and the income from interest is being spent on the consumption goods that are being produced. They are quite content. What about the number of workers who need jobs? (This point was picked out by Harrod in terms of a growing economy. The rate of investment that absorbs saving makes the employers quite happy, but the "warranted" rate of growth of the stock of capital which this produces is not in any way regulated to fit the "natural" rate of growth of the effective labor force.)

It is here that confusion between the two models very often occurs. The argument is switched back to the first model where the wage bargain can be made in real terms. When there is redundant labor, the real wage in terms of each commodity falls. It becomes profitable to employ more labor per unit of "capital"

---

[7] *Principles,* pp. 516–517.

up to the point where the marginal product of labor is brought down to equality with the lower real wage.

This argument falls between two stools. The "quantity of capital" is neither a list of stocks of fully specified means of production, as in the first model, nor a sum of value embodied in forms appropriate to the ruling rate of profit as in the second. No comprehensible explanation has ever been given of what it *is* supposed to be.

The highly unsatisfactory nature of these two models and the still more unsatisfactory mixture between them are generally concealed by elaborating analysis of their micro-properties—particular prices and so forth—which leaves their macro-outlines in a haze.

MARSHALL

The notion of the supply price of capital being the "reward of waiting" was invented by Marshall, but he never really reconciled himself to the confines of a stationary state. In his vision of contemporary capitalism, as opposed to his formal analysis, "progress" is taking place. He can best be understood if we set his argument in a kind of near-enough golden age with steady overall accumulation going on and a more or less constant overall rate of profit. Profits in particular industries go up and down around a central "normal" level, and the total stock of capital is continuously growing. This model, which we may label Marshallian, though it is only one element in Marshall's complex of doctrines, has something in common with the classics, since it depicts growth; but it is radically different in its theory of profits. For the classics, the real-wage rate is given in terms of the commodities that the workers consume; the rate of profit then emerges as a residual. For Marshall, the rate of profit is given and the real-wage rate in terms of all commodities emerges as a residual.

But then another flaw in the argument appears. In all the talk
in the *Principles* (as opposed to the formal analysis) it is not the
saving of rentiers but the energy of entrepreneurs which governs
accumulation. The individual businessman, with firmness and
elasticity of character, is striving to expand his own business and
in doing so adds to the national stock of productive capacity.
"The building of an additional floor on the factory or putting an
extra plough on one farm, does not generally take a floor from
another factory or a plough from another farm; the nation adds
a factory floor or a plough to its business as the individual does
to his." [8] In the famous passage [9] which anticipates Keynes, a
slump occurs when confidence fails—investment declines, unemployment reduces the demand for consumer goods and so
multiplies itself. Clearly it is the confidence of the entrepreneurs
in future profits that has failed, not the desire of rentiers to add
to their wealth. But if the rate of profit dominates the rate of
interest and the entrepreneur dominates the rentier, there is nothing in the story to say what determines the "normal" rate of
profit. Still less is there anything to provide the moral justification for rentier income that Marshall sought to derive from the
need to reward the "sacrifice" to capitalists of owning capital.

THE WICKSELL PROCESS

There is another kind of mixture of the two models which is
associated particularly with the name of Wicksell. In his story
the economy is stationary in the sense that there is no technical
progress, but saving is going on. The given state of knowledge is
embodied in a hierarchy of techniques of production which can
be arranged in order of levels of output per head and of "capital"
per man employed. There is full employment of a constant labor

---

[8] *Principles,* pp. 535–536. This is in contrast to the supply of "land,"
which is fixed.
[9] *Ibid.,* p. 711.

force and "capital" accumulates by installing successive techniques, moving up the hierarchy. The marginal product of "capital" is falling as time goes by and consequently the rate of interest falls. Equilibrium in the sense of the first model must mean that, at each moment of time, the stock of capital goods is adjusted, not to a single rate of interest but to the spectrum of interest rates appropriate to various lengths of future time, while equilibrium in the sense of the second model means that the rate of saving is appropriate to the expected return on rentier wealth. We have to imagine correct foresight of a complicated future development combined with the blind "groping" of Walrasian markets.

It is very difficult to find assumptions that will make this story self-consistent (Wicksell himself gave it up in despair) and it hardly seems worthwhile to do so, for the notion of accumulation and technical change without any evolution of technical knowledge is unnatural. In the progressive capitalist economies, adaptation takes place along with investment. There is no hierarchy of techniques already fully blueprinted—the blueprints are drawn only for the technique that will be used. Moreover, continuous accumulation is unlikely to be associated with a falling rate of profit. The problem of choice of technique is important for developing countries but for them the main point is to reach full employment in the first place. It is important also for fully planned socialist economies. For them, there is a "cost of waiting" in the sense that a project which will yield output at a later date is *pro tanto* less eligible than one yielding sooner. This concept can be expressed in a notional rate of interest to be taken into account in planning investment but a rate of profit on the existing stock of "capital" has no meaning for them.

There does not seem to be any place anywhere where the "Wicksell process" of accumulation under equilibrium conditions with a falling rate of profit has application. It was an attempt to integrate two incompatible models which are much better kept separate.

2

THE SHORT
PERIOD

Marshall discussed the influence of demand upon supply in terms of a succession of three periods or phases. When the supply of a commodity "is limited to the stores that happen to be at hand," demand alone determines price; next, productive capacity being given, demand may influence the rate of output over a certain range; finally, "in the long run" productive capacity is adjusted to demand and prices are governed by cost of production, including profit at the normal rate on the investment involved.[1]

The distinction between the first phase and the second is not very useful. As Marshall himself pointed out: "Nearly all dealings in commodities that are not very perishable, are affected by calculations of the future."[2] For manufactured goods of which retailers hold stocks, the concept of "market clearing prices" makes no sense. The second phase, however, introduces an invaluable concept, which sharply distinguishes the Marshallian school of thought from the tradition of Walras—that is, the "short period" during which the stock of plant is unchanged while its utilization can be varied.

---

[1] *Principles*, p. 337.
[2] *Ibid.*

16

This corresponds to the relations of production in capitalist industry. At any moment capacity is limited by buildings, equipment, and know-how already in existence. An industrial firm has committed finance to more or less long-lived installations on which it expects to recover a net profit over some years of operations. It is committed also to employing staff through contracts which cannot easily be terminated. On the other hand, ordinary labor can be employed week by week or even day by day and running expenses for power, raw materials, and so on vary with weekly output.

When closely examined, the distinction between a stock of plant and its degree of utilization, between variable and fixed costs or sunk costs and escapable costs, cannot be made quite precise. Some costs are sunk forever, some are necessary per week or per shift irrespective of the amount of output being produced; in a time of general scarcity of labor, a manager may be just as reluctant, when there is a fall in sales in his particular market, to stand off skilled workers (who may never come back) as to reduce staff. Similarly, the bottleneck that checks increasing output may be the availability of labor—especially of skilled manpower—rather than the existence of plant. But the general notion of a distinction between changes in utilization and changes in productive capacity is indispensable for the analysis of industrial activity.

The essential idea is that a short-period situation is one in which productive capacity happens to be whatever it is. But a situation with specific plant in existence today is not to be identified with the Walrasian concept of a given stock of factors of production; its role in analysis is quite different. Unlike the Walrasian concept, Marshall's short period is a moment in a stream of time in which expectations about the future are influencing present conduct, and it belongs to a monetary economy in which the division of proceeds between wages and profits emerges from the relation of money prices to money-wage rates.

With the aid of this concept, we can analyze price policy in imperfect competition, the effects in the present of uncertainty about the future, and the meaning of equilibrium in a process of growth, all of which are ruled out by the assumptions of a Walrasian market.

We can make use of the distinction between the long- and short-period concepts without being committed to any faith in equilibrium being established in the long run. Indeed, it is absurd to talk of "being in the long period," or "reaching the long period," as though it were a date in history. (Marshall himself thought of the economy as *tending* toward long-run equilibrium but never actually being there.) It is better to use the expressions "short period" and "long period" as adjectives, not as substantives. The "short period" is not a length of time but a state of affairs. Every event that occurs, occurs in a short-period situation; it has short-period and long-period consequences. The short-period consequences consist of reactions on output, employment, and, perhaps, prices; the long-period consequences concern changes in productive capacity.

SUPPLY PRICE

A short-period situation may or may not be in equilibrium from a long-period point of view. In a situation which is in equilibrium, no one is kicking himself. Expectations are being fulfilled. Plant, operated at a normal level of utilization, is producing a flow of output which is being sold at prices that promise to yield a satisfactory rate of profit on the investments concerned. Labor of appropriate skill and training is available to be employed. When a sudden unforeseen change has recently occurred, long-period equilibrium does not obtain; the stock of plant and the composition of the labor force are found to be inappropriate. They cannot be altered overnight but their utilization can be changed to make the best of the situation meanwhile.

An out-of-equilibrium situation may be a seller's or a buyer's market. In a seller's market, the level of demand is such that it would be possible to sell more than the capacity rate of output at prices that cover average total costs (including all overheads and an allowance for amortization) and yield a net profit. In a buyer's market, it is impossible to sell capacity output at a remunerative price. The distinction is not precise because capacity output is not a clear-cut conception. There may be an intermediate range of rates of output that cannot be classified unambiguously, but a rough-and-ready distinction is sufficient for the main argument.

The reaction of output and price to unforeseen changes in demand depends upon the competitive situation among the producers concerned. In some types of trade (mainly for agricultural produce) commodities are thrown on the market and sold for what they will fetch; but for manufactures it is the other way round—the producer declares a price and sells what the market will take.

Marshall assumed that a higher rate of utilization of plant would be accompanied by higher prices. In the Pigovian system this was systematized in the notion that, in conditions of perfect competition, the level of output is always such that marginal cost is not less than price, provided that the price covers average prime cost. If so, in a seller's market prices would be pushed up to the point where demand is cut back to equality with capacity output; in a buyer's market, high-cost capacity would be shut down and those plants kept in operation for which average prime cost was not greater than price. Then any plant that is working at all is working up to capacity.

The experience of an all-round buyer's market in the 1930s shocked us into realizing (what Marshall always knew) [3] that

---

[3] See *Principles*, p. 458.

prices may be held above prime costs and plants worked at less than full capacity; and the experience of seller's markets in recent times has shown that long delivery dates and rationing of customers accompany prices held below the level that chokes off excess demand. In short, imperfect competition is the general rule in manufacturing industry.

In modern industrial capitalism, market structures and the policies of sellers are very various. Where a single monopolistic firm has a strong hold upon a market, or where two or three powerful oligopolists are maneuvering in it, there is a great deal of scope for individual policy. In the general run of more or less competitive industries, the most common behavior seems to be as follows. Firms make their plans and calculate their average costs of production on the basis of a normal or standard rate of utilization of plant. Moderate variations of output above and below the normal level leave prices unchanged but a strong swing in demand, or a change in costs due, say, to a change in wage rates or in the price of a raw material, calls for a reconsideration of prices. When a number of firms are supplying the same market, no one wants to be the last to cut prices or the first to raise them, for fear of losing customers to competitors. From this the institution of price leadership arises. A convention is established that all await a change made by one firm and all follow it immediately. The leader pursues a policy that suits its own convenience, but it is in the position of a reigning monarch among baronies. Its independence is limited by the need to avoid offending the interests of the other members of the group. Moreover, disputes over the succession break out from time to time.

In a normal situation, the prices set by the leader enable it to make a comfortable rate of profit, while other firms, smaller in size, less efficient, or struggling newcomers, have higher costs and lower margins. In a buyer's market, the institution of price leadership prevents the competitors from cutting each other's throats; when costs rise, it enables them all to defend themselves from losses. In a strong seller's market, price leadership may have rather a tendency to keep prices down below the "perfectly competitive" level with a view to nursing the market through a period of shortage.

The best simple generalization seems to be that (so long as wage rates and the prices of the elements entering into prime costs are constant) moderate swings of demand have no effect at all on prices (the short-period supply curve is perfectly elastic). But this does not mean that they have no effect upon profits. With constant prices, the excess of receipts over costs is greater the higher the rate of output, for overhead costs are independent of utilization and even prime costs per unit may fall as output increases up to the limit where capacity is being strained. The *ex post* realized profit on an investment is higher the higher the average level of utilization of plant over its lifetime.

Moreover, there is a justification for Marshall's view that an increase in demand for the products of a particular industry will lead to an increase in prices, provided that it is believed to be strong enough to justify increasing investment in productive capacity; but this occurs not so much because marginal costs are pushed up as because the firms concerned consider that they need more profits to finance the investment, and that they are justified by proper business principles in exacting them, while they find them easy to earn in the conditions of a seller's market created by an expansion of demand ahead of the growth of capacity.

On the other hand, in a buyer's market, maintaining or even raising prices (as may happen under monopoly or strong price leadership) is unlikely to prevent profits from falling.

EXPECTATIONS

The third stage in Marshall's story of the adaptation of supply to demand is much less satisfactory. First, as we have seen, he does not give a comprehensible account of the level of the normal rate of profit which enters into the determination of prices "in the long run." Second, he seems to imply that, when new competition is attracted into a market by exceptional profits, it will increase capacity gradually until profits are reduced to the normal level. He fails to point out that, in such a case, there is likely to be an overshoot which causes profits to fall sharply, instead of sliding gently down to the "normal" level. Third, giving an optimistic account of the operation of the economy, he concentrates on the effect of a rise in demand leading to an increase in capacity, not of a fall causing it to shrink. Once investment has been made and businesses established, the process of reducing productive capacity is slow and painful. As Dennis Robertson used to say, the short period is not the same length at both ends.

The link between a short-period situation with given plant and the changes in productive capacity which will follow from it is constituted by the state of expectations generated within it.

When a process of steady growth is going on and expectations are being realized, the changes taking place at each moment are harmonious; they will lead to changes in the amount and the composition of productive capacity that fit with the development of demand.

Complete equilibrium is never found in reality, but it is approximated when plans are based upon long-term calculations. Fluctuations around the normal level of utilization of plant then have limited consequences. A boom is recognized as a boom. High profits are enjoyed without investment being speeded up; a fall of sales is weathered through as a temporary misfortune. Instability arises from the influence of current experience upon expectations. When a seller's market is expected to last, it leads to rapid investment which may cause an overshoot and kill the seller's market. But in a buyer's market, productive capacity is kept in being hoping for a recovery, so that if recovery does not occur, the buyer's market persists.

EFFECTIVE DEMAND

Marshall was discussing the demand and supply of particular commodities. The analysis is even more important when applied to the movements of effective demand as a whole.

In a harmonious situation, expectations are capable of being fulfilled. Productive capacity is growing at the same rate as demand in the markets that it supplies; the level of profits expected for the immediate future is inducing such a level of investment as will generate such a level of profits as will justify these expectations.

In a boom, expectations are self-contradictory. Profits are high because investment is going on, and investment is induced by expectations of profit which are due to that investment. Sooner or later, growth in the stock of productive capacity competing in the market will overtake growth in demand; the prospects of profit on a further increase in capacity are dimmed; a fall in the rate of investment then reduces actual profits.

A depression is a situation of self-fulfilling pessimism. Expectations of profit are low, therefore investment is discouraged, therefore sales are below normal capacity operation, therefore profits are low; therefore gloomy expectations are proving correct. (In trade-cycle theory, a revival grows out of a depression when the stock of equipment is reduced relatively to demand, just as the crises of a boom grow out of an overshoot, but it may be doubted whether an upturn ever occurs of itself, without some fresh external stimulus to effective demand.)

Keynes' General Theory arose from the attempt to diagnose

the situation of a general and prolonged buyer's market. The hard core of the analysis is concerned with a short-period position with given productive capacity and given expectations of future profits. This accounts for the paradox that what is strictly speaking a static theory opened the way to a great outburst of dynamic analysis. Keynes was concerned, above all, to show that there is no "natural" tendency toward equilibrium with full employment; therefore government policy is necessary to make the private-enterprise system work in a tolerable manner. He was, of course, mainly preoccupied with the question of remedies for unemployment; he merely glanced at the problems of inflation in a seller's market [4] and his long-period analysis was very sketchy. It was left to Harrod to transpose *The General Theory* into long-period terms, showing that an uncontrolled capitalist economy cannot be expected either to maintain stability or to produce growth at a satisfactory rate.

Since the Keynesian revolution became orthodox, the governments of all the advanced industrial nations have been very much concerned to preserve near-full employment for workers and highly profitable markets for capitalists. New influences are playing upon the movements of effective demand, which are outside the purview of Marshall, let alone the general equilibrium of Walras.

---

[4] He analyzed inflation later, in *How to Pay for the War* (London: Macmillan, 1940).

3

INTEREST AND
PROFIT

In an economy where manufacture is carried on by artisans, the earnings of labor, capital, and enterprise cannot be distinguished as separate sources of income. Skill, knowledge, work, business sense, and ownership of the appropriate means of production, bound up together, are supplying particular commodities to particular markets. In a competitive economy (where the regulation of just prices has broken down) the income to be made from a particular commodity is strongly affected by supply and demand. Social income is, so to say, divided vertically into receipts from separate commodities. When employment for wages becomes the main form of production, the division is horizontal, between income from work and income from property. Profit as a distinct category of income is a characteristic of industrial capitalism.

Marx, following the hard-headed classical economists, attributed profit to the power of capital to exploit labor. The neoclassicals rejected this point of view but they never succeeded in producing an alternative theory of profits that was both coherent and plausible.

WALRAS

When Walras introduced a rate of interest into his timeless, nonmonetary market, he gave two completely incompatible accounts of it, which, no doubt, he hoped would come to the same thing.[1]

In one story, there is a certain commodity which yields a return in the form of a perpetual annuity at some percentage rate upon its value. The hire-prices of all the physical factors of production are still determined by supply and demand in the market, but now the prospective earnings of each piece of property are capitalized at the general rate of interest so as to give its present value. Walras himself is rather vague about the capital value of a worker regarded as a factor of production. One of his latter-day disciples has the courage to carry his ideas to their logical conclusion, that is, to capitalize the future earnings of the labor force, so that prospective net national income is represented as a return equal to the rate of interest on the capital value of the total stock of factors of production.[2] But even he cannot suggest any way of accounting for what the level of this rate of interest is.

The second story in Walras is connected with saving. Every seller in the market immediately spends his receipts upon something but he is at liberty to buy means of production, say machines, which are valued for their future earning power. At any moment there are given conditions of production for each type of machine and the price of a machine, regarded as a product, is determined by supply and demand along with all the other commodities. The ratio of the current hire-price of a machine

---

[1] See *Elements of Pure Economics,* trans. W. Jaffe (London: Allen & Unwin, 1954), Lesson 23.

[2] See J. R. Hicks, *Capital and Growth* (Oxford: Clarendon Press, 1965), p. 264.

to its cost represents its current rate of return. The rate of profit is then established by the machine for which this ratio is highest. The prospective hire-price of other machines is capitalized at this rate. The value of all but the most profitable machine is then found to be less than its cost of production. Only the most profitable type of machine is worth having. The savers are buying machines of this type.

But Walras failed to point out that if savers are guided by current values they will be misguided. To make correct investments they need to know the future course of relative prices of all commodities and types of machine. This model also has been worked out in neo-neoclassical terms; [3] but it seems impossible to reconcile the contradiction between the assumption of correct foresight for each individual over an indefinite future and the daily higgling of a Walrasian market.

MARSHALL

In the Pigovian stationary state, which formalizes the static element in Marshall's system, the rate of interest is the return on the rentiers' wealth (the reward of waiting) which is just sufficient to induce them to keep it in being. Finance is lent and borrowed, in indefinite amounts, at this rate. Consequently the prices of commodities and the allocation of resources between different uses are such that every investment of capital earns a rate of profit equal to this rate of interest. Such a theory is quite hollow; it merely repeats the assumption that in a stationary state, the rate of profit is equal to the reward of waiting.

In Marshall's account of a growing economy there is a great deal of verbal confusion between various meanings of the rate of interest. In his terminology, the long-term rate of interest is

---

[3] Cf. M. Morishima, *Equilibrium, Stability, and Growth* (Oxford: Clarendon Press, 1964), Section III.

identified with the rate of profit on capital and this, in turn, is sometimes, but not always, identified with rentier income (the reward of waiting). On the other hand, the short-term rate of interest or rate of discount is a phenomenon of the money market; it can be influenced by the behavior of the banks or by movements of the supply of gold.[4] (Wicksell similarly distinguishes between the "natural rate of interest," which means the rate of profit and the "money rate of interest," which is the cost of borrowing.)

The terminology can be revised as follows. Profit is the net return to a firm on its invested capital. Interest (a complex of rates for various types of loan) is the hire-price of finance; the yield of placements is the rate of return that a rentier receives on the capital value of his assets.[5] The last two are connected, for the rate of interest in the money market influences the secondhand value of placements, but the range of transactions that they cover is not identical. An important element in the complex of interest rates is the charge for bank loans (in Marshall's day, the rate of discount on bills); from the point of view of a bank, interest on loans is one part of its gross receipts, not a return on capital, while rentier wealth may include elements such as real estate not corresponding to the liabilities of business firms. In all this, the most important point is to isolate Marshall's conception of the rate of profit on capital.

At any moment, investment is going on; firms already in existence are planning to enlarge their productive capacity and new businesses are being started up. Investors, looking into the future, reckon what prices they can expect for additional output and what wages and other costs they will have to pay, and they

---

[4] Cf. E. Eshag, *From Marshall to Keynes* (Oxford: Blackwell, 1963), Chapter III.

[5] Of course, in reality the "reward" of owning wealth is owning wealth, whether or not it yields income; the "reward" of saving is an addition to wealth.

know what additional equipment a given sum of money can buy at current prices. They thus calculate the rate of profit to be expected on investment. (This may be expressed either as the rate of discount which reduces the value of the expected gross profits spread over future time to equality with the present cost of investment, or as the permanent annuity that the investment could secure by amortization and reinvestment, maintaining the capital intact over an indefinite future.) Each investor goes in for the scheme that promises the highest return. In normal times, for the representative investor, expected prices and costs (here is the missing link in the argument) will work out so as to give an expected yield on the investment equal to the "normal rate of profit." Marshall insisted that the rate of profit (which he called the long-term rate of interest) can be seen only at the frontier of investment, looking forward, but if "normal" conditions normally obtained, the actual realized rate of profit would generally turn out to be equal to the expected rate. There is a tendency for the rate of profit to be evened out throughout the economy: or rather there is a pattern of profit rates—lines which are easy to enter on a small-scale may have a lower rate of profit than that enjoyed by the great firms; or within one industry, at a moment of time there may be struggling or decaying firms doing badly compared to the "representative firm" which at that moment is in its prime. (As an observation of contemporary family businesses, Marshall's story of "trees in the forest" was apt, although its role in his theory was not convincing.)

The diffusion of profits throughout the economy is maintained by the short-period mechanism. Where demand is expanding ahead of supply in some line, prospective profits are seen to be high. Not only a large proportion of new investment will flow in that direction, but also amortization funds from less successful lines. Thus the push and pull of demand are continually molding the stock of capital into the form which yields the normal return.

The value of all capital goods in existence today is found by capitalizing their current net earnings at a rate corresponding to the normal rate of profit. The rate of interest which is paid on borrowed finance normally accommodates itself to the expected rate of profit, with an allowance for risk; but it may be influenced by monetary factors which displace it from its proper level. When the rate of interest is too low, speculation sets in, rash investments are made, prices are driven up. Too low a rate of interest thus causes a temporary and unhealthy rise in prospective profits. It was left to Keynes to point out that too high a rate of interest causes depression and low profits.

In this part of the argument, Marshall has tacitly abandoned the idea that the rate of profit is equal to the reward of waiting, for, if it were, investment would not be going on. And the influence of the monetary rate of interest on the rate of profit is only an unfortunate aberration. So what does determine the normal rate of profit? Marshall evidently hoped that his readers would not notice that he does not say.

KEYNES

Keynes cleared up the verbal confusions of the neoclassics by drawing a sharp distinction between the rate of profit and the rate of interest, that is, between the return on real investment accruing to entrepreneurs and the cost of borrowing which influences the return on secondhand placements received by rentiers. But he did not attempt to supply a theory of the rate of profit in the long run. His argument was concerned purely with a short-period situation. The expected rate of profit, which he called the marginal efficiency of capital, is an estimate of future returns to be obtained on investments in productive capacity; it is necessarily uncertain and it is influenced by subjective psychology— the state of the animal spirits of the investors.

The actual rate of profit being earned on the capital already in existence has no meaning in the short-period situation that

Keynes was discussing. The overall total of gross profits per annum is whatever it is; it cannot be reduced to net profit without knowing the future in order to calculate what depreciation should properly be deducted from it; furthermore, the *rate* of net profit involves a calculation of the value of capital; the historic cost or the current reproduction cost of stocks and equipment are irrelevant; they reflect past conditions, not the future. The value of the stock of capital, in this situation, can mean only its expected future earnings discounted at some appropriate rate. If we knew what the rate of profit was, we could use it as the rate of discount, calculate the value of capital, and show that it is yielding the rate of profit. But this in no way helps to find out what the rate of profit is.

The complex of yields which represents return on capital from the rentier point of view is determined by the interplay of the preferences of owners of wealth and the stocks of money and various other kinds of placements (bonds, shares, etc.) in existence. The level of prices is established from day to day in the market. The monetary authorities, through the banking system, can influence the level of interest rates by operating on the supply of money.[6]

It is clear enough that a fall in the rate of interest (in a given state of expectations) raises the capital value of all income-bearing placements, of real estate and of house property which yield rents in cash or in kind; it cannot have any direct effect upon the value today of equipment being used in industrial production. It may have an important influence in stimulating house building and lowering future rents; its effect on industrial investment is not so clear (except that small businesses may find it easier to get bank loans). On this point Keynes rather lost his grip on the distinction between the rentier and the entrepreneur.

---

[6] Cf. below, p. 79.

His discussion of "the state of long-term expectations" is devoted to the Stock Exchange rather than to the accumulation of means of production.

Where he allowed his mind to play upon long-term problems, his conceptions are still more obscure. In particular, the suggestion that the euthanasia of the rentier could be brought about merely by establishing a permanently low rate of interest nowadays seems fantastical.

THE NEO-NEOCLASSICS

The neo-neoclassics,[7] who tried to reconstruct traditional orthodoxy after the Keynesian Revolution, slipped back into the habit of identifying the rate of profit with the rate of interest and reasserted the doctrine that the rate of return measures the marginal productivity of capital from the point of view of society as a whole, without attempting to explain what it means.

The neoclassical scheme of ideas was intended to present an industrial economy as a scene of rationality and social harmony under the guidance of the "hidden hand" of competitive market forces. Marshall had some reservations; the clearest statement came from J. B. Clark. "What a social class gets is, under natural law, what it contributes to the general output of industry." [8] On this view, the profit received by the capitalist is due to the contribution to output of his capital. Capital equipment contributes to output (along with education and training) by raising the productivity of labor; a command of finance permits a capitalist to provide equipment, employ labor, and receive profits. The neo-neoclassical revival of pre-Keynesian theory took over J. B. Clark's identification of capital as profit-earning finance

---

[7] See, in particular, R. M. Solow, *Capital Theory and the Rate of Return* (Amsterdam: North Holland Publishing Company, 1963).

[8] "Distribution as Determined by the Law of Rent," *Qualitative Journal of Economics* (April 1891).

with capital as a stock of means of production. Leaving land on
one side, "capital" and labor are the "factors of production"
and their "rewards" correspond to their "marginal productivities." [9] The basis of this doctrine seems to be a confusion between the idea of the productivity of investment and the productivity of "capital."

The Productivity of Investment The productivity of investment to society is not a very precise idea but it has an important
meaning. We can imagine an independent peasant family, or a
cooperative society like a kibbutz, deciding how much of their
labor to devote to improving the land or how much of the proceeds of sales to a surrounding market economy to devote to
buying productive equipment. The cost of an investment is more
work or less consumption in the present and the benefit is an increase in the productivity of work in the future. Neither the cost
nor the proceeds are homogeneous and both contain psychological elements; the relation between them can be represented
as a rate of return only by adopting some more or less arbitrary
convention of measurement. However, the general idea of a
present sacrifice yielding future advantages is clear enough.[10]
What has it got to do with the rate of profit on capital? In such
a community, the current output of consumption goods, and the
future benefit of higher consumption or more leisure, will be
distributed among its members on some principle or other; the
means of production belong to the community as a whole and
the distinction between income from work and income from
property has no meaning for them.

Under laissez-faire capitalism, the division of net output between consumption and investment is decided for society by
profit-seeking entrepreneurs. There is no mechanism in the sys-

[9] This proposition is categorically reaffirmed by C. E. Ferguson in
The Neoclassical Theory of Production and Distribution, p. 215.
[10] Cf. Solow, p. 154.

tem even to ensure that all available labor is employed for one or the other. When there is unemployment, the cost to society of some additional investment is not much more than zero, indeed it is negative if we bring the misery of unemployed workers into the account, but capitalists would have to pay wages to get it done.

In a progressive near-full employment economy, maintaining a growing national income with a more or less constant rate of profit, the *effective* labor force is evidently increasing through growth of numbers and rising output per head (otherwise growth with a constant rate of profit would not be possible). The product from the point of view of society of the investment which is going on includes the growth of the real-wage bill as well as the additional profit. If this is the "marginal product of capital" it much exceeds the rate of profit. In order to know how the benefit to society will be divided between wages and profits in the future we need to know the rate of profit; there is nothing here to tell us how it comes to be what it is.

In one sense, modern capitalism has something in common with a cooperative where the benefit of investment is set against its cost. A government may consider that near-full employment has been achieved with too large an amount of consumption and too little investment for the future good of the economy. The government then wants to make the market for consumption goods less profitable and investment more attractive. It finds it by no means easy to do so, for to reduce the profitability of the market discourages investment, but one way or another it may succeed. It is being guided by some general view of national interest, which might perhaps be expressed in terms of the productivity of investment but has nothing to do with the rate of profit on capital.

The Pseudoproduction Function　Another deep-seated confusion arises from failing to distinguish between comparisons of stocks of capital in imagined equilibrium positions and accumulation going on through time, such as the Wicksell process of "capital deepening." [11] (Both are very unreal concepts but it is necessary to set them up in order to see what they are intended to mean.)

In a Pigovian stationary state, with a given rate of interest, we are to suppose that there are a number of different possible methods of producing a given rate of output; competition between profit-maximizing firms has led to capital being embodied in forms which yield a rate of profit equal to the rate of interest. On this basis we can construct a pseudoproduction function showing all the possible points of equilibrium in an imagined "given state of technical knowledge" which is intended to illustrate the supposed effect of relative "factor prices" (the real-wage rate and the rate of profit) on the choice of technique. The techniques are set out in order of net output per man employed. At each rate of profit, the eligible technique is the one which permits the highest real-wage rate to be paid when that rate of profit obtains. Any method of production which is not eligible at some rate of profit is *inferior* and is not included in the schedule of techniques. For each pair of techniques there is a rate of profit at which they are equally eligible. One technique requires a higher value of capital per man than the other (at the prices corresponding to that rate of profit) and produces a net value of output per man just sufficiently higher to pay the additional profit required; with a small difference in the rate of profit, one or the other ceases to be eligible.

It was in this context that the "reswitching" controversy arose. At labor-value prices, the cost of equipment required for each technique is proportional to the labor-time required to produce

---

[11] This confusion is very clearly seen in Professor Samuelson's "Summing up" of the "reswitching" controversy. "Paradoxes of Capital Theory," *Quarterly Journal of Economics* (November 1966).

it. A higher real-wage rate then entails a higher cost of capital per man employed. A technique with a higher cost of capital cannot be eligible (at any rate of profit) unless it has a higher output per man. Thus, in such a case, the order of techniques in terms of capital per man is the same as the order in terms of output per man. The pseudoproduction function then looks like the "well-behaved production function" of the neo-neoclassics, on which an *addition* to "capital" per man produces an addition to output per man. The switches of techniques on the pseudo-production function are then always *forward,* a lower rate of interest causing a technique with a higher output per man to become eligible.[12]

But, as Ricardo realized, labor-value prices are a very special case. They rule only when the capital to labor ratio and the time-pattern in which costs are incurred are the same in all lines of production. In the general case, the rate of profit as well as the real-wage rate enters into relative costs; since the two move in opposite directions (a lower rate of profit entails a higher real-wage rate) the cost of the equipment required for any one technique (in terms of a unit of net output) may rise or fall with the rate of profit. Over a range where the cost of the equipment for the technique with the lower output per man rises with the rate of profit by sufficiently more than for the adjacent technique with a higher output, there will be a *backward* switch, so that a higher wage rate is associated with a more "labor intensive" technique, that is, with a lower output per man. For the neo-neoclassicals this was a paradox. It upsets the notion of a production function exhibiting substitution between labor and "capital."

---

[12] This was the case of Professor Samuelson's famous "Surrogate Production Function." It was actually a special form of the pseudoproduction function. See "Parable and Realism in Capital Theory," *Review of Economic Studies* (June 1962).

This analysis provides a very striking illustration of the fact that the old neoclassicals had failed to give a definition of a "quantity of capital" (except for the case where it can be measured as "labor embodied," which was not to their fancy) and it shows that the concept of the "marginal product of capital" is unseizable; certainly, at a switch point, comparing one technique with another, profit per man is proportional to the value of capital per man, so that, in a certain sense, the return on investment is equal to the rate of profit. But this is true only because all prices of inputs and outputs are such that the rate of profit is the rate corresponding to that switch point.[13]

But the whole argument is only negative. Such a thing as a pseudoproduction function does not exist in nature. There is no sense in arguing about whether it is "likely" to be well-behaved or not, and however perfectly well-behaved it might be, it could not tell us anything about how the rate of profit comes to be what it is.

The pseudoproduction function appears to be important only when it is confused with an actual production function which shows how investment made today will affect output in the future.

Wicksell (though he abandoned the attempt) at one time tried to make use of a simplified pseudoproduction function (in which techniques are specified only by the length of the "period of production") to find the relation between the rate of profit (which he called the natural rate of interest) and the "marginal product of capital." According to this line of thought, the stock of means of production in existence today operating techniques now known came into existence by embodying savings made in the past. The Wicksell process of accumulation in a "given state of technical knowledge" requires a rise in "capital" per man,

---

[13] Cf. L. L. Pasinetti, "Again on Capital Theory and Solow's 'Rate of Return,'" *Economic Journal* (June 1970).

going on through time to be associated with a falling rate of profit. Thus, accumulation is seen as creeping along a production function which was always known and does not alter as the process goes on. Suppose that ever since Adam left paradise a single state of technical knowledge has obtained and investment has been slowly increasing the stock of capital. Then as the rate of profit falls, technology must gradually pass each switch point at which two techniques are equally profitable and at each point the return on investment is equal to the rate of profit.

This is evidently absurd. If we were to take the story seriously, we should have to suppose that the stock of capital at any moment has been chosen in the light, not of one rate of profit, but of a complex of rates corresponding to different periods of future time. And we would have to suppose that the stock of capital equipment at any moment was not embodying a single technique appropriate to a particular set of prices and rate of profit, but was composed of fossils of past investments made in the light of expectations of higher rates of return than those now ruling.

No doubt it is perfectly possible to work all this out on stated assumptions, but such an analysis does not even pretend to apply to either the past or the future of the economy that we are living in.

RICARDO AND VON NEUMANN

While the neoclassical tradition was running into the sand, there was a revival of interest in the classics.[14] In the classical theory of the rate of profit, the real wage is treated as part of the necessary costs of production.

In Ricardo's corn economy, the output of corn produced by a man-year of work on marginal land is a technical datum. The corn-wage is also a technical datum, given by the needs of subsistence. Output minus wage is the annual profit per man employed. The wage rate and the length of time from harvest to harvest determine the corn-capital required to employ a man. Profit per man over capital per man, each as a quantity of corn, is the rate of profit. The rate of profit emerges from the technical data of the system because the necessary wage is part of the specification.

The rate of profit being determined in the production of the wage good, competition sets the corn-prices of all other products so that they yield the same rate of profit. The corn-value of the output of a man in any industry, minus the wage, provides a gross profit per man employed which is sufficient to keep capital intact and to yield the standard rate of profit on the corn-value of the capital goods associated with employing him. Ricardo himself was mainly interested in the prospective fall in profit per man employed as increasing total employment extended the margin of cultivation. Moreover, he was distracted by the objec-

---

[14] This was being carried out mainly under the influence of Piero Sraffa. His article of 1926 which set off the theory of imperfect competition, his preface to Ricardo's *Principles* (1951), and finally the *Production of Commodities by Means of Commodities* (1960) constitute a criticism of the theory of distribution in terms of marginal productivity which the neo-neoclassics have not been able to answer, though they have attempted to dodge it by arguments such as those described above.

tion that the real wage cannot be treated as a single homogeneous product into giving up the corn model and pursuing the
will-o'-the-wisp of an "invariable measure of value." [15]

After being lost to sight for a century, the pure classical
theory of profits was worked out by von Neumann.[16] In his
model, the necessary wage consists of a specified basket of commodities. These commodities are produced by labor with the aid
of a stock of commodities—equipment, raw materials, and the
like—all of which are produced within the system by labor and
themselves. The commodities are combined in the proportions
which produce the fastest maintainable growth rate of the output
of baskets of wage goods. As the flow of output of wage goods
increases, employment of labor grows (either the population is
growing at just the right rate or there is an indefinite reserve
of potential labor, living on nuts in the jungles, ready to take
employment when the standard real wage is offered). In any
period, the surplus of production over the wage of the labor
employed and the replacement of the means of production used
up constitute net profit. The physical elements in the net profit
are in the same proportion as the stock of means of production
and the wage paid. Thus the ratio of net profit to the stock of
capital is unambiguous. The technical conditions of production
and the real wage determine the rate of profit.

There is an element in the von Neumann model which might
be taken to suggest a resemblance to Walrasian marginal productivity. It is physically possible to produce some or all of the
commodities with various proportions of others. The optimum
proportions are characterized by marginal productivities equal
to prices. But at any point on a von Neumann path, the optimum

---

[15] See Piero Sraffa, Preface to Ricardo's *Principles. Works and Correspondence of David Ricardo* (Cambridge: 1951), Vol. I.

[16] See "A Model of General Economic Equilibrium," *Review of Economic Studies,* XIII (1) no. 30 (1945–1946).

proportions for the whole output have already been chosen; the stock of means of production already exists in the correct proportions. All relative prices are appropriate to costs of production including profit at the standard rate. This is totally different from the Walrasian situation where stocks of commodities, means of production, and labor are given, at any moment, in arbitrary proportions and relative prices and wage rates are settled by supply and demand. Von Neumann's equations describe the equilibrium conditions of an optimum path; they cannot, in the nature of the case, say anything about what happens to an economy when it is out of equilibrium.[17] Nor does von Neumann say anything about the pseudoproduction function. His economy is bound to the one technique dictated by the real-wage rate. (If the wage rate were specified in calories instead of quantities of particular commodities, we might compare economies where the workers were fed, say, with wheat or with potatoes. In the latter, the real cost of the wage would be lower and the rate of

---

[17] When a planning authority is provided with a job lot of means of production and wishes to maximize employment at some future date, it has a wide choice of possible policies even if it is confined to a single technology. At one extreme, it might find the bottleneck commodity, collect a set of inputs in the optimum proportions from the stocks available, discarding the surplus amounts of those in more than the optimum ratio to the bottleneck commodity, and set output growing at the maximum rate. (This is the "turnpike" policy.) At the other extreme, it might begin by producing only the bottleneck commodity until there was enough of it to make some other the bottleneck, and so on, until the stock had been built up to the optimum proportion with the commodity of which there was the largest supply (relative to requirements) in the original job lot. Which policy within this possible range would be best must depend upon the detailed specification of the original stocks of commodities and the technical equations. There cannot be an a priori assumption that the turnpike policy will be eligible. This way of looking at things, of course, is leaving out the main problem that arises in reality. In von Neumann's world, labor comes into existence only when there is a real wage to feed it. Actual planners are worried about workers who already exist.

profit higher. The relative prices of all commodities would be different in the two cases, and different techniques of production might be eligible.)

Von Neumann assumed that the whole surplus was continuously being invested in enlarging the stock of commodities and increasing employment. Then total net profit and total net investment are identically the same thing. The rate of profit is equal to the rate of growth.

Let us vary his assumptions by supposing that owners of property consume part of the output of wage goods. The rate of profit and the level of wages cannot be affected, for they are fixed by technical conditions. The rate of growth would be reduced. Here is an important clue which will be picked up later.

THE RATE OF EXPLOITATION

In Ricardo's corn model, profit is pure exploitation. The workers have to seek employment because they have no access to land and no means to live from harvest to harvest. The function of the capitalist is to engage to pay rent to the landlord and to advance corn-wages to the workers. He is taking advantage of their necessity to make them produce a profit for him.

But this exploitation is not to be deplored. It is the only way that wealth can be increased. The landlords consume their share of the corn in supporting feudal retainers. The capitalist consumes very little of his share; he invests it in employing more workers and producing more profit.

Marx enlarged the conception of accumulation through exploitation. Competition between capitalists drives them to reduce costs by increasing output per head so that they "ripen the productive power of social labor as though in a hot-house."

In Volume I of *Capital,* Marx seems to predict that, as capitalism develops, real wages will fluctuate around the level which was established when industrial employment first began to take over from an economy of artisans and peasants. As output per head increases, with constant wages, the rate of exploitation is rising. The tension between rising production and constant or falling consumption for the mass of the population will bring an explosion. But in Volume III there are hints of a different prognosis, according to which the rate of exploitation will tend to be constant. If so, the real-wage rate must be rising in step with output per head.[18] The diagnosis of Volume I seems to fit with modern experience in the so-called developing countries where the level of wages at which capitalist investors can recruit labor is kept low by the supply of would-be workers with no means to live; the share of profit in proceeds in the enclaves of modern industry is extremely high.[19]

On the other hand, in the successful industrial economies, where near-full employment prevails, where trade unions are strong, and social legislation aims to eliminate desperate misery, it seems that a fairly constant rate of exploitation tends to be established so that a rising overall level of real wages becomes normal. This (up till now) has saved capitalism from the contradictions that Marx expected would destroy it, both by fending off the indignation of the workers and by keeping a market expanding for goods and services that can be profitably supplied to them.

Once we remove the postulate that the real wage is technically determined, the classical theory of profits loses precision; but it

---

[18] Marx believed that the development of technology must be such as to raise the ratio of capital to output. Then, if the share of profit were constant, the rate of profit must be falling. In modern conditions, it seems, there is a tendency rather to keep the value of output per man employed and the value of capital per man rising more or less in step, so that a constant share of profit in net output and a constant rate of profit in capital are not incompatible.

[19] Cf. P. J. Loftus, "Labour's Share in Manufacturing," *Lloyds Bank Review* (April 1969).

still provides the basis for an account of how the system operates.

SAVINGS AND INVESTMENT

Let us return to von Neumann's model and alter his assumptions in two respects; there may be a certain range of real-wage rates in terms of larger or smaller baskets of commodities and the whole net profit need not be invested in expanding the system—part may be consumed by rentiers.

Now, if we compare two paths with the same real-wage rate and the same techniques in use but different proportions of profit consumed, the rate of profit (as we saw above) is the same in both; the growth rate in each is equal to the rate of profit multiplied by one minus the proportion of profits consumed. When the whole net profit is consumed, the growth rate is zero. (This is a kind of stationary state that has some features in common with the Pigovian model.)

Then (at a point where total employment is the same on both) compare two paths (having the same technique) with equal proportions of profits consumed, but one with a higher growth rate than the other. The latter has a higher rate of profit.[20] Its real-wage rate is lower for two reasons: first, the proportion of investment to consumption is higher; second, the

---

[20] If we release the assumption of a rigid technique, the higher rate of profit and lower real wage may be supposed to have led to the selection of different techniques from the spectrum of possibilities which is in common for the economies being compared. The technique which is eligible at a higher rate of profit may have either a higher or a lower output of a given basket of commodities per unit of labor. (This proposition was established in the double-switching controversy.) When the pseudoproduction function is well-behaved, a higher rate of profit is associated with a lower output per head, which lays a further burden upon the workers. (This proposition is derived from the golden rule or neo-neoclassical theorem. See below, p. 136.)

amount of profit being greater, the amount of consumption by rentiers is greater. Or, if we compare two paths with the same growth rate, that which has the lower proportion of profits consumed has the higher real-wage rate.

These propositions are summed up in the formula, when

$$s_w = 0, \pi = g/s_p.$$

π is the rate of profit on capital, g is the rate of expansion of the economy, s_w and s_p are the proportion of saving in wages and profits respectively. In the classical theory, the real wage is fixed and profit emerges as a residual, depending upon technical conditions; in this theory, the rate of profit is determined by the combined effect of saving and investment, and the real wage emerges as a residual.

All this is merely a set of formulae. The question at issue is how the allocation of labor and means of production between investment and consumption is carried out under laisser-faire capitalism. Is it, as the classics thought was obvious, the industrialist who invests and ploughs back profits to expand his business, or is it (as the neoclassics seemed to maintain) the householder who decides how much of his income to consume and hands over the rest to be invested?

In writing the *General Theory* it took Keynes a "long struggle to escape" from the neoclassical view but much earlier he had described the system flourishing before 1914 in classical terms:

Thus this remarkable system depended for its growth on a double bluff or deception. On the one hand the labouring classes accepted from ignorance or powerlessness, or were compelled, persuaded, or cajoled by custom, convention, authority and the well-established order of Society into accepting, a situation in which they could call their own very little of the cake, that they and Nature and the capitalists were co-operating to produce. And on the other hand the capitalist classes were allowed to call the best part

of the cake theirs and were theoretically free to consume it, on
the tacit underlying condition that they consumed very little of it
in practice.[21]

Under capitalism, from the first, the function of profits was
to be saved and saving, in the main, took the form of investing
the profits accruing to a business in its own expansion. Some part
of profits was handed over to the households of the capitalists
or paid as interest to those who provided finance, but if the main
purpose of profit had been to support rentier consumption "the
world would long ago have found such a regime intolerable." [22]

Adopting the classical view, we can supply the missing link
in the Marshallian model. Firms are carrying out schemes of
investment with a view to increasing their operations. Earned
and unearned incomes (in the language of the British Inland
Revenue) are being paid out to households, and money is flow-
ing back from households to firms for the purchase of goods and
services.

If we postulate that the budget is balanced and that any net
saving out of earned incomes is offset by private house building,
it follows that the overall sales value of the goods and services
being bought by households from firms, over any period, exceeds the wage bill directly and indirectly incurred in producing
them by the amount of the wage bill for new investment plus
expenditure out of profits (in which should be included the
greater part of the salaries that the captains of industry allow to
themselves). Here is the source of net profit. The equivalent of
the prime costs of production of goods sold to the public is
recovered from expenditure of their own wage bill; gross profits
are recovered from the wage bill of the investment sector and

---

[21] Keynes, *Economic Consequences of the Peace*, pp. 16–17 (London:
Macmillan, 1919).
[22] *Ibid.*

expenditure on consumption out of profits. Setting off amortization against the cost of replacements, net profit is equal to the value of net investment plus the value of rentier consumption. As Kalecki puts it, the workers spend what they get and the capitalists get what they spend.[23]

Technical conditions and the level of profits determine the level of money prices relatively to money-wage rates and so determine the level of real wages in terms of any basket of commodities.

A surplus or deficit in the foreign balance on income account is added to or set off against home investment. A deficit in the budget and an excess of house building over saving from earned income tell in the same direction as net investment (a surplus in the budget or in saving from earned income reduce net profit correspondingly).

All this is concerned with actual flows of payments. The *rate* of profit which governs investment plans is not an actual payment. It is an expression of expectations of future prices and costs. Only when an economy is growing smoothly in the conditions of a golden age, with expectations being continuously fulfilled and therefore renewed, does the realized rate of profit have a definite meaning. The conditions of our formula are then fulfilled. Profit is generated in the sale of consumption goods (just as, in the corn economy, it is generated in the production of the wage good); the rate of profit obtainable in industry in general enters into the prices of investment goods that firms sell to each other or into the book value of those that they produce for themselves. The rate of profit (when there is no net saving out of earned income) is equal to the rate of accumulation divided by the proportion of profits saved.

Reality is never a golden age. There are disturbances due to

[23] Cf. below, note 8, p. 119.

markets in which supply and demand rule, mistaken expectations, and unforeseen events. The rate of profit on capital is neither uniform throughout an economy nor steady through time. Nevertheless, the concept of the normal rate of profit determined by investment and the propensities to save provides the framework of a general theory within which detailed analysis can be built up.

The normal rate of profit must be sharply distinguished from the rate of interest. The reward of waiting—the rate of return on rentier wealth—is determined in the money market. With the facilities that modern institutions provide, marketable placements are much less risky than productive assets; the level of their yields is normally much below the prospective rate of profit that attracts real investment.

The function of legal and financial institutions, including the Stock Exchange, is to reduce lenders' risk and so facilitate the supply of finance to industry. Nowadays the major part of industrial investment is financed from retained profits, and no doubt this was just as much the case in the era of Marshall's family businesses as it is under the regime of managerial capitalism. At the same time new businesses are always being started; family concerns are being sold to the public and issues of securities may be made by firms who prefer to finance expansion that way. There is therefore a need for outside saving as well as retention of profits. On our assumptions, the overall rate of outside saving is equal to the excess of investment over retentions, but new savings are not necessarily directly available to be borrowed. A small trickle of new demand for placements and money is coming at any moment into the large pool of the capital market from savers and a trickle of new issues is draining it off. The level of prices of the whole pool of securities is constantly changing with the "state of the news." To see the influence of the supply and demand of finance, we can imagine that we are examining the market in a state of tranquillity when

a stable rate of profit and rate of growth are confidently expected
to continue to be maintained for an indefinite future. For the
level of interest rates to remain constant then requires that the
pattern of growing demand for placements is matched by the
pattern of supply; in particular, it requires the banking system to
allow the quantity of money to expand to satisfy the liquidity
preference of the owners of the growing total of wealth (as well
as the needs of trade) and, one way and another, to make the
loans to industry which the rentiers do not provide. Thus, when
the demand for securities is growing more slowly than the supply, the level of interest rates will be tending to drift upward
unless the movement is offset by the banking system, and contrariwise.

Self-finance of firms increases the rentiers' wealth as well as
their own savings. Provided the investments financed out of
retentions are successful, they increase the earning capital of the
firm. In a family business, the family may claim a right to enjoy
the benefit; in a public company, the value of shares rises. Insofar as this increase in their wealth stimulates rentier consumption, it tends to raise the overall level of the rate of profit on invested capital.

The above provides Marshall with the basis of a theory of the
rate of profit and the rate of interest, but it does not provide
what he was looking for—a justification for rentier income.

EFFECTIVE DEMAND

Keynes reproached the classical economists (whom he did
not distinguish from the neoclassicals) with neglecting the problem of effective demand. Ricardo conceived that the workers are
obliged to consume their wages in order to live; the landlords
consume their rents and the capitalists either consume or invest
their profits. There is no possibility of a breach between supply
and demand because the product is distributed in real terms.

In the corn economy there is no specialization and exchange so there is no problem of finding a market for whatever is produced.

Marx paid some attention to the problem of "realizing surplus value"; the product of his business accrues to a particular capitalist in the form of some particular commodities; they must be sold before the proceeds will pay his wage bill and provide his profit. Marx repudiated Say's Law and in some passages he suggests that underconsumption will be the doom of capitalism. In the main line of his argument, however, the capitalists are always investing the surplus that comes into their hands so that the problem of realization solves itself.

Rosa Luxemburg maintained that the capitalist system can keep up its rate of investment (and therefore its profits) only so long as it is expanding geographically. Marshall allowed for the possibility of a collapse of confidence [24] but he did not lay much emphasis on it and his pupils were propounding the truth of Say's Law and the Treasury View at the time when they were struck by the great slump.

Keynes diagnosed the flaw in the laissez-faire system that allowed such a disaster to occur. Since the war, governments in all capitalist countries have been playing a large part in their economies and they have succeeded for some time, mainly by high levels of expenditure largely financed by budget deficits, in maintaining near-full employment and creating a situation favorable to a high overall rate of profit.

Avoiding slumps is all to the good as far as it goes, but now there is growing up, especially in the United States, a protest against the wasteful or pernicious lines of production into which government and industry direct resources, and their failure to provide for the basic human needs of the population. The neo-

---

[24] See *Principles*, pp. 710–711.

neoclassical economists cannot take any part in this great debate as long as they have nothing to contribute to it except the tattered remnants of the laissez-faire doctrine that what is profitable is right.

4

INCREASING
AND DIMINISHING
RETURNS

The expression "increasing and diminishing returns to scale" implies some kind of symmetry between these phenomena but in origin they have nothing in common. The notion of diminishing returns was developed from Ricardo's theory of rent; increasing returns, from Adam Smith's principle that the division of labor depends upon the extent of the market.

The classical economists were concerned with a process of historical development. A number of confusions and contradictions have arisen from the neoclassical attempt to squeeze their concepts into the mechanical equilibrium of a stationary state.

The concept of constant returns to scale, in the technical sense, means that each physical input required for a given output —man-hours of labor of specific skill and energy, machines of specific types, materials, sites, and so forth—can be regarded as homogeneous within itself, and that a given proportionate increase in each input will bring about an equal proportionate increase in output. Diminishing returns arise from the fact that some inputs, in particular those that are given by nature, cannot be increased at will. To produce a certain proportionate increase in output then requires a more than proportionate increase in *other* factors. There are still conditions of constant returns in a technical sense; *if* all factors were increased, output would increase in the same proportion. On the other hand, the economies of large-scale production which give rise to increasing returns operate by changing the nature of the inputs. Output per man-hour grows as work becomes more specialized; equipment can be designed to produce a larger output at lower cost, larger supplies of materials can be more finely graded, and so forth. It is not a question of the proportions in which given physical inputs are used but rather a question of the specification of the inputs themselves. When some inputs have to be provided on a large minimum scale—say a railway network—strictly constant returns can be realized only for increases in output which are a multiple of the capacity of the indivisible inputs. For ranges of increases in between there are increasing returns due to sub-optimal utilization of the input. (To make the Walrasian system work we have to assume divisibility of all factors—otherwise the services of some items would fall to a zero price just after they had been built at great expense.) This concept is logically distinguishable from the economies of specialization but the two are likely to be mixed up together in any actual case.

The main difficulty about these conceptions is connected with time. A change (in output, in prices, or in costs) is an event, taking place at a particular moment, that alters the situation in which the change took place.

IRREVERSIBILITY

The notion of a functional relationship between output and costs can make sense only in strictly short-period analysis. When the specification of inputs and of methods of work remains unchanged from year to year, output may rise and fall, as more of variable inputs are applied to one that is fixed, up and down a supply curve which remains independent of the direction of change. Such conditions may be approximately fulfilled when the amount of output of a particular crop depends upon the application of man-hours of work, over a yearly cycle, to a particular area of agricultural land. There must have been irreversible investments made in the past in clearing the land, in drainage, irrigation, and so forth; but once the investment has been made, productive capacity is kept intact in the course of operating it, so that henceforth investment is indistinguishable from the "natural resources" in which it is embedded; the short-period situation is quasipermanent. Similarly, in industry with given equipment, output per head may fall or rise as older plant is bought into or put out of use.

But a long-period supply curve is a very treacherous concept. To *increase* productive capacity requires investment. The larger capacity will exist at a later date than the smaller capacity which preceded it. In general it will be different in its technical nature, for three reasons. First, technical change is continually going on in the industrial economies. New plants will embody techniques formerly untried. Second, the mere fact of expanding capacity involves technical adaptations even when they are applications of general principles already known. (The notion of a "book of blueprints" exhibiting "the state of technical knowledge" has played a part in doctrinal controversy, not in realistic analysis. In reality techniques are blueprinted only when they are about to be used.) Third, large installations often require investments of a quasipermanent type which alter the whole situation forever after.

Marshall was uneasily aware of the problem of irreversibility. He thought of an *increase* in output as taking place through time. A lower point on his falling supply curve is at a later date. When output has once expanded from A to B, a retraction of output back to B would take place at lower costs than obtained when B was the rate of output in the first place.[1] This was a way

---

[1] See *Principles,* Appendix H.

of smuggling technical progress, learning by doing, and irreversible investment into the static theory.

The most important example of this way of thinking was the "infant industry case" as an exception to the presumption in favor of free trade. It is sufficiently obvious that when one country is trying to catch up upon the advanced technology of another, it must protect its industry from lower-cost competition until it has cut its teeth. In the process of development the scale of industry may grow but the main point is not the scale but the *time* that it takes for workers and managers to learn the business and for accumulation to provide the installations that it requires. Since there was no room for time in the neoclassical model, the argument had to be framed in terms of economies of scale. This, like Marshall's irreversible supply curve, is an example of common sense breaking in and thereby wrecking the logical structure of the equilibrium model.

Economists have not much emphasized the opposite kind of irreversibility—the destruction of resources, the devastation of amenities, and the accumulation of poison in air and water. Pigou made a great point of "external diseconomies" such as the smoke nuisance but, within the confines of his stationary state, he could not emphasize *permanent* losses. It has been left rather to the natural scientists to sound the alarm, while orthodox economists, unperturbed, continue to elaborate the presumption in favor of laissez faire.

"MARGINAL PRODUCTS"

A second problem presented by the concepts of diminishing and increasing returns, was concerned with the relation of "marginal products" to factor prices. In the Walrasian stationary state, the higgling of the market and recombination of factors are supposed to settle all marginal productivities and all hire-prices by a simultaneous process. There is, in a certain sense, a rising marginal cost for each commodity; if the output of any one commodity were to be increased, it would have to attract factors of production from other uses so that their price in terms of the commodity in question would have to be raised. But such an increase in output is only notional. When the supplies of all factors of production are given, output of one commodity can increase only if other outputs are reduced. A change in the pattern of demand means that some factors of production are released, where demand has fallen, to be transferred to the production of the commodities for which demand has risen. Before we can say what happens to the price of a commodity of which output rises, we must know what specific factors of production are released by the fall in output of other commodities.

To find the marginal product of a specific factor, say a certain type of machine, we have to consider what output would be lost if a unit of this factor were withdrawn. This loss is the reduction in output of the commodity that this machine was used to make minus the increase in output of other things due to deploying the labor and other factors cooperating with the machine in other uses. The physical marginal product is thus a very complex entity, while the value of the marginal product has no unambiguous meaning, since the pattern of prices, of factors and commodities, is altered by the change in productive capacity. Thus it is hard to understand what is meant by saying that a factor (say a park of machines of a particular type) receives a reward (say, the hire-price per machine year) [2] equal to the value of its marginal product.[3]

Marginal product in Ricardo's scheme has a quite different

---

[2] We have to assume that machines do not require amortization for it is impossible to distinguish gross and net product in Walrasian terms. Cf. above, p. 10.

[3] Cf. below, pp. 68–69, for the definition of marginal productivity in a one-commodity economy.

meaning. In the simplest form of Ricardo's model, the only output is "corn," which stands for all agricultural produce, and it is the only wage good. Capitalist farmers are accumulating corn in order to expand future output. To employ a man from harvest to harvest requires a specific investment of corn—the wage fund—which is equal to the wage bill for a year. Labor and capital are inseparable—the unit of input is a man-year of work together with the investment of corn in advancing a year's wage. Capitalist farmers maximize profits by deploying labor in such a way as to equalize the intensive and extensive margins of cultivation, that is, so that the additional output of corn from adding a man-year of work on the best land is not less than can be obtained by increasing the area of cultivation (neglecting the cost of breaking in new ground). Thus marginal product per man-year falls as employment and output expand over successively less fertile land. (Rent absorbs the difference in the productivity of better and worse land, so that the farmer receives the same average return for each man he employs.) Now, the marginal product of an additional man employed provides the wage per man-year *and* the profit on the capital required to employ him. It is far from being the case that each "factor" separately receives its marginal product. Man-plus-capital earns the marginal product (which is equal to the product of a man-year of work on marginal, no-rent land). The wage-bill for the man-year is deducted from this product and what remains is the profit on the capital required to employ a man. The principle remains the same when capital includes equipment and stocks of materials, though the problem of valuation is then not so simple as when output and capital are made of the same stuff.

In Ricardo's scheme, the corn-wage was fixed by the needs of subsistence, so that as output per man (net of rent) was falling, the rate of profit on capital was being eroded. If we like to postulate a constant rate of profit on capital, then, in such a case, the real wage would be falling with the marginal productivity of a man-plus-capital as total employment increases.

Marshall understood the difference between marginal productivity in Ricardo and in Walras but he made it very difficult for his readers to see the point.[4]

ECONOMIES OF SCALE

The application of the idea of marginal productivity to the case of increasing returns caused even more trouble. Marshall thought of the economies of scale as mainly internal to an individual firm operating a single plant. There were also external economies due to the development of an industry as a whole. He did not think of any limit to economies of scale. "As the industry grows, the firm grows." Thus (at constant money-wage rates) cost per unit of output was a decreasing function of output. But he maintained that prices are equal to average cost including an allowance for normal profit. Thus prices must fall with costs. However, for each firm, marginal cost is less than average cost; therefore less than price.

This was Marshall's famous dilemma.[5] How can competitive conditions be reconciled with increasing returns?

Pigou tried to rescue Marshall by postulating an optimum size of firm at which long-period costs are at a minimum. Then, to enjoy normal profits, the firm must be working beyond the point of minimum cost to just such an extent that the excess of marginal cost (which is equated to price) over long-period average cost is sufficient to yield the required profit.[6] When price is

---

[4] Cf. above, p. 12.

[5] Cf. G. L. S. Shackle, *The Years of High Theory*, p. 11 et seq. (Cambridge: 1967).

[6] The equilibrium price can be presented as equal to minimum average cost by including a lump-sum normal profit per annum in total cost. In

higher and output is greater than this, supernormal profits are attracting in new competition and forcing the firm back. Contrariwise when output is less. To make room for increasing returns, Pigou then had to rely upon purely external economies, or "economies of large scale to the industry." Each firm was always working under conditions of rising marginal cost, but an increase in the number of firms would lower average cost at the minimum for all of them. (This is a simplified account of an intricate argument which was broken off before it was resolved.) [7] This fanciful construction, although it was demolished by Piero Sraffa more than forty years ago, is still used as the basis of the "theory of the firm" in modern textbooks.

The next problem was to introduce the "laws of returns" into a theory of the relative prices of commodities.

In the Walrasian stationary state all supplies of factors are physically specified and fixed in amount. Each pattern of demand then produces a particular pattern of relative prices. (In the P.O.W. camp, if there were a larger proportion of Sikhs, who do not smoke, the cigarette prices of other items in the parcels would generally be higher.) [8] Pigou did not think of physical factors (except "land") as being specified and fixed; nor did he go to the other extreme (which came into fashion after his time) of thinking of the stock of capital equipment as a large lump of putty. He did think of the total of "resources" as being somehow given.

Formalizing Marshall's vague suggestions, he identified in-

Wicksell's version of this argument, profits are zero in equilibrium so that price is equated to minimum cost to the firm. See *Lectures* (London: Routledge, 1934, vol. 1, p. 26). But for Wicksell the rate of interest enters into costs of production. Cf. below, p. 97.

[7] See "Increasing Returns and the Representative Firm: A Symposium," *Economic Journal* (March 1930).

[8] Cf. Radford, "The Economic Organization of a P.O.W. Camp," *Economica* (November 1945).

dustries with commodities, and he divided the industries into those where diminishing returns predominate, so that the supply price of the commodity is rising with output, and those where economies of scale to the industry predominate, so that supply price is falling.

A change in the pattern of demand would release "resources" from some commodities to be embodied in means of production for other commodities. This put into his head the idea that to reduce the output of commodities "subject to diminishing returns" and transfer resources to commodities "subject to increasing returns," by a system of taxes and subsidies, would bring about an increase in total real output and in welfare. However, he soon recognized that this was based upon a false symmetry between increasing and diminishing returns.[9] A reduction in demand for a commodity produced with the aid of a scarce factor reduces the rent of the factor. This is a transfer of wealth, not a saving of cost to society.

Abstracting from scarce factors, what remained of the argument seems to be as follows. Each commodity is produced by a competitive industry which sells it at a price corresponding to its cost of production including normal profits. Some commodities are more susceptible to increasing returns than others, so that if "resources" were moved between industries to take advantage of the difference, the loss of economies of scale in those where output was reduced would be less than the gain where output was increased. The pattern of demand is strongly affected by relative prices (in general, commodities are substitutes for each other) so that demand would be shifted by taxing some

---

[9] Pigou revised the argument originally put forward in *Wealth and Welfare* after the error was pointed out by Allyn Young in his review of the book (*Quarterly Journal of Economics,* August 1913). In successive editions of *The Economies of Welfare,* it became more incomprehensible at each attempt. *Wealth and Welfare* was published in 1912, the first edition of *Economics of Welfare* in 1920, and the fourth in 1932.

commodities and subsidizing others (the net revenue being zero). Total money income is given (there is full employment of workers at constant wage rates and a fixed total of "waiting" receiving a given rate of interest). The price to the consumer of taxed commodities would be raised by little, if anything, more than the tax (because they have little economies of scale to lose) while the price to the consumer of the subsidized commodities would be reduced by more than the subsidy, because of the gain of economies. Thus the real income of consumers would be increased.[10]

This argument was never treated seriously as a recommendation for policy and nowadays it seems to have dropped out of the canon of orthodox teaching. Pigou put it forward as an example of the theoretical exceptions to the rule that perfect competition, in conditions of laissez faire, produces the optimum distribution of given resources between alternative uses. Here again common sense was breaking in, but he managed to catch it and wrap it up in the assumptions of static equilibrium before it could do much harm.

All these difficulties and confusions connected with the concepts of diminishing and increasing returns arise from the neoclassical attempt to escape from time. When we set the argument in what I have called the Marshallian model—a growing economy with a constant normal rate of profit on capital—they appear much less intractable. Irreversibility is no problem. Time marches in; there is no need to pretend that the past is the same thing as the future. In the Marshallian model, the dilemma between competition and falling costs disappears. If the normal rate of profit is constant, as the economy expands, it follows that as output per head rises, money prices fall relatively to money-wage rates. By assuming a constant rate of profit Marshall has

[10] Cf. R. F. Kahn, "Notes on Ideal Output," *Economic Journal* (March 1935).

assumed that prices are kept in line with costs; competition may be highly imperfect, in the sense that each firm has considerable freedom in setting prices; the number of independent firms in any one market may be falling; but still the economy is competitive in the broad sense; all he needs is to assume that firms generally prefer to take advantage of falling costs to expand sales rather than to try to hog a monopolistic profit by restricting the growth of output.[11] In this model there is no great importance to be attached to the distinction between economies of scale and technical progress, nor between economies internal to a firm, economies accruing to an industry producing a particular commodity or economies resulting from the general development of industry, transport, distribution, and finance.[12] As time rolls on, output of all kinds is increasing; productivity rises more for some commodities than others and relative prices alter accordingly. So long as the rate of profit on capital is constant through time, long-run normal prices are governed by costs. The forces of demand—the distribution of purchasing power, needs and tastes of the consumers, and persuasive skill of salesmanship—influence the composition of output. The only effects of demand upon prices arise where there are bottlenecks created by specialized factors of production in limited supply which cannot be broken by technical innovations or where economies of scale are concentrated upon a particular commodity. Only thus does the composition of output react upon costs of production and so on relative prices. Supply-price rising and falling with the sale of output of particular commodities then appears as a quite minor complication. (Marshall, it seems, puffed it up out of all proportion in order to bring supply and demand into the forefront of his doctrines.)

---

[11] Cf. below, p. 102.

[12] The last type of economies was the subject of the famous address of Allyn Young, "Increase Returns and Economic Progress." *Economic Journal* (December 1928).

But once we bring historical time into the argument, it is not so easy to present the free play of the market as an ideal mechanism for maximizing welfare and securing social justice. Marshall himself admitted that accumulation and employment depend upon expectations of an uncertain future. His short-period theory is a theory of instability and in historical terms his theory of distribution based on "rewards" of "factors of production" becomes meaningless. Economic history is notoriously a scene of conflicting interests, which is just what the neoclassical economists did not want to discuss.

5

NONMONETARY
MODELS
Much of traditional doctrine is set out in terms of an economy which operates without money, implying that the "real" system is operating behind "the veil of money" which the economist must tear aside. Money, however, in this view is not only a veil, it can somehow interfere and distort the real relations which would obtain without it. The main point of this doctrine is that, in a market in which all transactions are conducted in kind, supply creates demand, goods are the demand for goods, so that without money there could never be underconsumption or overproduction; there could never be involuntary unemployment or underutilization of productive capacity.

But what does the absence of money entail? The Walrasian model is not only without money, it is without time. Goods are exchanged against goods "today." Prices are set at the level that clears the market so that there is no carryover to tomorrow. The essential characteristic of the model is not the absence of money but the absence of any effect of expectations about the future on present behavior.

MARKET PRICES

In an actual market, even the simplest, a trader sells for the sake of acquiring purchasing power that he can use later—hours or years later as he pleases. Any durable good that is expected to be in fairly general demand in the future provides a vehicle for purchasing power. Clearly it is a great convenience to all concerned when some particular commodity is recognized as a general medium of exchange; [1] when convention has endowed a commodity with general acceptability the demand for it in its capacity as money overshadows its direct use. Trade has ceased to be swapping of goods for goods; demand is divorced from supply; equilibrium is not guaranteed. Money then gets the blame for the fact that the future is uncertain.

As we know very well from experience, an equilibrium price will be established when dealers know what the equilibrium price is. (The leading case of this phenomenon was the operation of the gold standard before 1914.) A chance fall in price today below the equilibrium level is quickly corrected by buying for stock; a chance rise, by running stocks down. Production is carried on in the knowledge of what costs it is worthwhile to incur. When dealers have to *guess* the future course of prices, a fall today often leads to selling, causing a further fall, and contrariwise. Producers take time to adjust supplies; an increase in demand leading to a high price is followed by an excessive increase in output that cracks the market. Uncertainty, not money, is the cause of the trouble.

There is a quite different sense in which the Walrasian model is nonmonetary, that is, there is no general price level. Each seller is interested in the purchasing power of his own particular

---

[1] Cf. R. W. Clower, *Monetary Theory, Penguin Modern Economic Readings* (London: Penguin Books, 1969), pp. 9–14.

product over particular things that he wants to buy. But this, which should be the strongest point in Walrasian analysis, generally seems to be smoothed over in expounding it. The model is used to show that a competitive equilibrium has the characteristic that (with given supplies of physical factors of production and a given list of products) no more could be produced of any one thing without producing less of another. This is described as an optimum position. An increase in the supply of any one product moves the system to a superior position. But superior from whose point of view? This must be looked at.

Let us suppose that, after a position of equilibrium has been established, there is an increase in the supply of one commodity, say peanuts, others remaining unchanged. The peanut price of other commodities is raised. A new equilibrium is established in which the distribution of income among the traders is affected by the change in prices that has occurred. When the elasticity of demand for peanuts in terms of things in general is unity, the sellers of peanuts purchase the same total of goods as before while the rest of the traders purchase more peanuts. (There may be changes in the relative prices of other commodities and changes of income among the sellers of peanuts.) When the demand is elastic, the sellers of peanuts purchase more of other commodities. (Provided that there are no inferior goods for which demand falls when real income rises, the direction of a change in the quantity of commodities in general is unambiguous.) Now the rest are getting more peanuts and giving more of their own products, that is, they are consuming less of each others' products. The sellers of peanuts (taken together) are better off. Some of the rest, for whose commodities peanuts are a substitute, are likely to be worse off. When the demand for peanuts is inelastic, the sellers of peanuts are worse off. They are giving more peanuts for less of other commodities. The rest (taken together) are better off.

Where supply and demand rule in the modern world, that is, in trade in primary products, demands are generally highly inelastic. A good harvest may be a disaster—the farmer hanged himself in the expectation of plenty. Moreover, of course, the instantaneous re-establishment of equilibrium after a change in supply is a myth. The rest of the trading community does not necessarily gain from a sharp fall in the income of one group of producers. When a large part of the market for British textiles was in the colonies, a fall in the price of tea or cocoa caused unemployment in Lancashire.

All this has nothing to do with the existence of money. Conflicts of interest are a necessary characteristic of a system in which value depends upon scarcity.

The Walrasian system claims to provide a theory of general equilibrium while it is often said that Marshall with his one-at-a-time method provides only partial equilibrium. In fact, Walras provides only half a system for he discusses the prices of commodities without discussing the incomes of the people who trade them. The Pigovian model (for what it is worth) is a general equilibrium system though, like the Walrasian one, it is concerned only with comparisons of equilibrium positions, while the Marshallian system is more general than either, for it permits the discussion of processes going on through time.

A ONE-COMMODITY ECONOMY

A quite different kind of nonmonetary model is set up in terms of an economy with only one commodity. There are no relative prices—supply and demand have nothing to bite on—but net output per annum of the community is divided into income from work and income from property. In Ricardo's corn economy, the wage rate is fixed as a quantity of corn. (If wages were actually paid in bags of corn, corn would fulfill one of the most important functions of money.) The wage fund which reappears every year at harvest time as a quantity of corn is both physical capital and value of capital. The excess of the year's output of corn over replacement of capital and consumption is the year's saving which is added to the stock of capital for investment in expanding employment over the coming year. There can be no deficiency of demand and there is no problem of finding an outlet for investment; more workers, in Ricardo's world, are always available to take employment when offered the standard corn-wage. The model eliminates instability and uncertainty in order to concentrate on one problem—the distribution of the product of industry between the classes of society. The elimination of money is incidental to the elimination of uncertainty.

The neo-neoclassicals also make use of a one-commodity world. In their model, capital as a wage fund is neglected. (They want to say that the marginal physical product of labor is equal to the wage, not to the wage plus interest on working capital.) Capital is a stock of physical means of production. We can adapt the corn model to these requirements by supposing that the wage bill is paid in arrears out of the year's harvest and by introducing seed corn which is owned by capitalist employers. Land is a free good. There is a well-behaved production function in labor-time and seed corn. At the beginning of any cycle of production there is a stock of seed corn available to be invested and a labor force available to be employed. Competition, not only between workers for jobs, but also between employers for hands, ensures that the wage rate is set at the highest level that is compatible with full employment. The wage, that is to say, is equal to the marginal physical product of labor—the output that would be lost if one less man were employed, with the same total amount of seed corn. The return per ton on the stock of corn is then equal to its marginal product, that is to the output that would be lost if a small amount, say one ton less of seed, were used with the same amount of labor time, minus the replacement of the ton of corn.[2]

---

[2] It is usual to appeal to Euler's theorem to demonstrate that the marginal products, multiplied by the respective amounts of the factors, add up to the total net product. (See, for instance, Wicksell, *Lectures*

The special features of this construction are, first, that any given quantity of physical capital can provide employment for any amount of labor (the elasticity of substitution between them is positive over an indefinite range—the production function never cuts the axes of the diagram in which it is drawn) and a change in the ratio of capital to labor can be made without any cost of adaptation.[3] Second, the wage bargain between a worker and an employer is made in terms of his own product. Third, investment consists in adding something to a heap of means of production that already exists without requiring any change in it.

This model was constructed to provide a bridge between the conception of the stock of capital as a set of physical inputs which assist labor to produce output and as a fund of finance which enables the employers of labor to make profits. The bridge breaks when the peculiar assumptions of the one-commodity world are withdrawn from under it.[4]

The one-commodity assumption makes it possible to *define*

---

vol. I, pp. 127–128). In the corn model, the point can be simply shown. When one less man is employed, a quantity of seed corn equal to the average used per man is released and reallocated to the remaining labor force. The marginal product of labor is equal to the average net output per man minus the net addition to output due to the seed corn released, that is, minus the marginal product of corn multiplied by corn per man. Total net output is equal to the marginal product of labor multiplied by the quantity of labor plus the marginal product of seed corn multiplied by the quantity of corn. We take, as the unit of the quantity of each factor, the unit in which marginal productivity is expressed. Here we take a man-year of work as the unit of labor and a ton as the unit of seed corn.

[3] In many neo-neoclassical models this conception is applied also to technical progress. For instance: "Capital is made up of a large number of identical meccano sets which never wear out and can be put together . . . to incorporate the latest technical innovations in successive editions of the Instruction Book." T. W. Swan, "Economic Growth and Capital Accumulation," *Economic Record* (November 1956).

[4] Cf. L. L. Pasinetti, "Switches of Technique and the Rate of Return in Capital Theory," *Economic Journal* (September 1969).

the marginal product of labor; the other assumptions, in particular indefinite substitutability of factors and a chronic scarcity of labor relative to demand for it, are necessary to support the proposition that wages tend to equal marginal products.

Even with all these provisos it is still not true to say that the return per unit of capital corresponds to the marginal product of investment from the point of view of society as a whole.

Consider a Wicksell process of accumulation of capital with a constant labor force, in the setting of the corn economy. Every year some part of the net output of corn is saved and added to the revolving stock of seed to be used next year. According to the rules of the model, seed corn per man employed is higher next year, net output per man is higher, though in a smaller proportion, the corn-wage is higher, and the return per ton of corn is reduced. Now compare the situations at two dates between which an appreciable addition has been made to the stock of corn. At the later date the permanently maintainable net output of corn (with a constant amount of work) is higher than at the earlier date by some number of tons per annum. This increment of output may be described as the product of the investment. In the corn economy the productivity of investment (which is in general both complex and vague) [5] can be neatly expressed as the ratio of the increment net output to the increment of the stock of seed corn brought about by investing the savings made over the period.

Each year the return per ton of seed corn is equal to the marginal productivity of the stock in existence. This rate of return is lower at the second date, and the level of wages is correspondingly higher. Total net income at the second date is equal to the income at the earlier date plus the increment which represents the product of investment. In respect to the level of income of

---

[5] Cf. above, p. 33.

the earlier date, the workers get exactly what the owners of seed corn lose; the increment of income also is divided between wages and profits in shares appropriate to the new position. Thus the increment of income due to the investment that has been made consists partly of wages.[6] At each point in the process of accumulation, the rate of profit (equal to the marginal product of corn-capital) is less than the product of the investment made over the past period.

In discussion of this subject, starting with Wicksell himself, and continuing to the present day,[7] there is much confusion between comparisons of positions of equilibrium corresponding to different rates of profit (a pseudoproduction function) and the effects of accumulation as a process going on through time; and between the return enjoyed by owners of wealth (the reward of waiting) and the productivity of investment from the point of view of society as a whole. The assumptions of the one-commodity economy enable us to sort out these distinctions, though it is more often used to confuse them.

MONEY AND "REAL FORCES"

These models are nonmonetary in the strict sense that they purport to operate without a medium of exchange. It is not possible to set up a nonmonetary model, in this sense, for an industrial economy. Where workers do not own the means of production that they operate and where there is specialization there must be money in the sense of some vehicle for general

---

[6] This was the original meaning of the 'Wicksell Effect' (see C. G. Uhr, "Knut Wicksell, a Centennial Evaluation," *American Economic Review,* December 1951). I borrowed this term, perhaps illegitimately, for the difference in the value of a given physical stock of capital goods at different rates of profit.

[7] Cf. above, p. 15.

purchasing power in which wages are paid.[8] The models of Marshall, Wicksell, and Pigou are monetary in this sense but, in the orthodox teaching which Keynes had to attack, "money" was used in a wider and vaguer sense. There was a dichotomy between "real" forces which determine the relative prices of commodities and factors of production and "monetary" forces which are responsible for the general price level and for movements of the national income as a whole. Thus "money" had both a wide metaphysical sense, as something opposed to what is "real," and a precise narrow sense as the actual monetary arrangements operating through the supply of gold and the institutions and policies of the banking system. Thus the orthodox doctrine (though rarely precisely stated) implied that the "real" forces establish equilibrium while aberrations such as inflation and unemployment are "the fault of money" and could be avoided by a correct policy of the monetary authorities.

The relation between monetary and real forces was expressed by Marshall in terms of the discount rate and the long-term rate of interest and by Wicksell in terms of the money rate and the real rate of interest. (As we have seen, the long-term or real rate of interest is identified with the rate of profit on capital.) The argument can be set out in terms of what I have called the Pigovian model—a stationary state in which the rate of interest is governed by the reward of waiting—that is, in which it is set at such a level that the rentiers are willing to own just the amount of wealth that is in existence. The system is monetary in the sense that a medium of exchange is in use but the mone-

---

[8] A model such as that set up by von Neumann or Sraffa does not need to mention money. All relative prices are determined by technical conditions and the rate of profit. Wages can be expressed in physical terms (though they could equally well be expressed by a money-wage rate and a level of money prices). But these models are systems of equations expressing equilibrium relationships. They cannot be used to discuss the behavior of the human beings who inhabit them.

tary system cannot have any permanent effect upon any of the real relationships within it.[9]

In the Pigovian stationary state, the rate of profit is equal to the rate of interest governed by the reward of waiting. The money-wage rate and the rate of profit determine all prices (given technical conditions) and the money value of national income and of total wealth. The supply of the medium of exchange is equal to the demand for it. Let us call this the supply of *cash*. The theory of real and money rate of interest is then set out as follows. Suppose that, in a position of equilibrium, cash is arbitrarily increased without any change in income having occurred. The redundant cash cannot find holders at the current level of prices. Consequently the price of interest-bearing bonds is bid up. Now the rate of interest has been reduced below the equilibrium level. Rentiers are getting less than the reward of waiting and they are holding a larger nominal total of wealth. They start to draw on capital to increase consumption; at the same time the entrepreneurs, finding the rate of interest lower and the rate of profit higher because of the increased demand for goods, want to increase investment. The two sectors, competing against each other for labor, drive up money wages. Wages and prices rise until the demand for cash has risen to absorb the extra supply at the equilibrium rate of interest. (Both Marshall and Wicksell told the story this way round. They did

---

[9] Before Keynes, there was a great deal of confusion in the neoclassical scheme as to the effect of the wage bargain on the distribution of income. Pigou himself was converted only after a struggle to the view that a change in money-wage rates primarily affects money prices, not real wages. (See "Money Wages in Relation to Unemployment" *Economic Journal,* March 1938.) Yet this was in fact essential to his own scheme. If prices are equal to marginal costs, an all-round rise in money-wage rates, which raises all marginal costs proportionately, must cause a corresponding rise in money prices. It was a mistake in terms of his own model to suppose that the wage bargain is made in real terms.

not remark that a *rise* in the rate of interest does not bring money-wage rates *down* in the rapid and painless manner that the argument requires.)

This way of arguing, however, is not legitimate. The stationary state is essentially timeless. It is not equipped to deal with unexpected events. It can be used only for comparisons of equilibrium positions. All that we can say on the basis of this analysis is that, in Pigovian stationary states, there is one stock of cash appropriate to each level of money-wage rates. When the wage rate and the stock of cash are not in harmony, the system is not in equilibrium.

MONEY IN A GOLDEN AGE

The argument can be extended to the model of steady growth with a normal rate of profit constant through time. The effective labor force is growing at a steady rate and entrepreneurs, one with another, are causing accumulation to take place at the same rate. The wage bill in terms of money is rising at the same rate. When the growth of effective labor force is only a growth of numbers, money-wage rates are constant; when output per head is growing, money wages rise in step so as to keep the price level constant. (Technical progress is neutral in Harrod's sense, so that the ratio of the value of capital to the value of output is constant.) The supply of cash must be increasing at the same rate as the wage bill. This comes about automatically if firms are financing the difference between this month's investment and last month's saving by borrowing from the banks and the banking system is allowing the supply of cash to expand appropriately. The proportion of household income saved is constant and so is the proportion of profits retained by firms to finance investment. In each period, household savings being placed by the purchase of securities, together with retained profits, are sufficient to finance the investment of the last period. The increase from one period to the next in the value of investment being met by borrowing from the banks, the quantity of money is growing at the same rate as the money value of the stock of capital. The rate of interest is constant and the supply of finance grows with the demand for it.

This is not a system in equilibrium; there is no mechanism to keep it on its path. The only point of setting it up is to see where it is liable to go wrong.

"REAL" INSTABILITY

The sources of disturbance in the golden age are not confined to the operations of the monetary system. Keynes broke down the old dichotomy; he showed that the "real" forces can by no means be relied upon to establish equilibrium, however well the monetary system behaves. The monetary system may, indeed, contribute to disturbances, and monetary management may do something, though not much, to dampen disturbances due to other causes, but it has a minor influence, either for good or ill. Supply and demand in the sphere of commodity trade; the instability of investment in uncontrolled private enterprise; the interplay of money-wage rates and money prices; these are the sources of disturbances. If the "real" forces were behaving properly, it would not be difficult to get the monetary system to work properly too.

The old dichotomy still haunts modern theory. It has been revived in a curious form by the Chicago school.[10] The argument is that when the national income, in real and money terms, is growing smoothly at a steady rate, it is found that the stock of money is growing at the same rate (at least a definition of

---

[10] See Milton Friedman, "The Role of Monetary Policy," *American Economic Review,* March 1968, reprinted in *The Optimum Quantity of Money* (Aldine Press, Chicago, 1969).

money can be found that makes this true). Therefore, to cause the stock of money to grow steadily is all that is necessary to ensure steady growth in the national income. The nonmonetary theory, that the real forces tend to establish equilibrium, thus reaches its apotheosis in the doctrine that money is the only thing that matters.

6

PRICES AND
MONEY

The archetypal quantity theory formula, $MV \equiv PT$, like any identity, has to have its terms defined in such a way as to make it hold. Keynes' identities, $Y \equiv C + I \equiv C + S$; $S \equiv I$, have the great advantage that they correspond to columns in the national accounts, income, consumption, investment, and saving. (The formula comes right because Y, I, and S are all net of depreciation, and the budget and the foreign balance are either boiled in appropriately with S and I or set out separately.) Keynes, in fact, embraced the modern system of national income accounts [1] in order to be able to convince his critics that $I = S$, not $S + \Delta M$. The elements in the quantity equation are not so transparent. M must be defined as the quantity in existence at a moment of time of a specific list of items, say, coins, notes, and bank deposits (whether inclusive or current accounts only). T is an index of transactions—is it to include all transactions made during a year, or only those connected with the production and distribution of the real national income? Similarly, P, an index of prices, must be appropriate to the list of transactions.

---

[1] See *General Theory*, pp. 102–103 and *How to Pay for the War*, appendix by E. Rothbarth.

Then V, the velocity of circulation of the money included in M, can only mean PT/M. Alternatively, if M includes all kinds of money used in connection with the transactions listed in T, and V is the average of the number of times that each item is used in a year, then M is PT/V. The so-called Cambridge equation, $M/P = kR$, where R is "resources" (presumably, an index of real income) and k is the ratio of money balance to "resources," was even more vapid—it only says that the real value of the stock of money is its nominal value divided by an appropriate index of prices.

The truisms are intended to be used, in a looser way, to exhibit causal relationships, like $\Delta Y = \dfrac{1}{s}(\Delta I)$,

where s is the marginal propensity to save. If the quantity equation had been read in the usual way, with the dependent variable on the left and the independent variables on the right, though rather vague, it would not have been silly. Suppose that, between one year and the next, PT rises; either activity has increased—employment and output are higher this year than last, or the general price level has risen because of a rise in costs in money terms; then if the quantity of money has not increased, the velocity of circulation must have risen. But it was not taken so. It was used as the basis of the argument that a change in the quantity of money will produce a more or less proportionate change in the price level.

I do not think that its supporters ever really believed it, for, if they had, they would have joined the money cranks in the great slump and proclaimed: "It can all be done with a fountain pen."

The reason why the equation was read left-handed was that it grew up side by side with a body of doctrine couched in "real" terms which consisted mainly of an exposition of the conditions of equilibrium. Employment, accumulation, real wages, and the production and consumption of commodities were looked after in Volume I of the *Principles of Economics,* and there was nothing left to discuss in Volume II except the supply of money and the general price level.

THE THEORY OF INTEREST AND MONEY

Keynes sloughed off the quantity theory in several stages. In the *General Theory* he emerged in a shining new skin. To find the determinants of the general level of prices, he now maintained, we must look first to the level of money-wage rates; the level of effective demand is a minor influence which he was inclined to believe in, though it was not essential to his argument.[2] The volume of transactions varies with the level of effective demand, and the principal determinant of changes in effective demand is changes in the level of investment.

Money plays a secondary role. The quantity of money is controlled by the banking system. When effective demand is beginning to rise, it induces an increase in average overall velocity of circulation as money balances are moved from the inactive to the active circulation. If the banking system fails to allow the quantity of money to increase, the demand for active balances will tend to raise the level of interest rates, which causes V to rise to the required extent—for instance, rentiers are induced to exchange holdings of money for bonds when the yield of the latter rises. In a period of unemployment, an increase in the quantity of money can do some good. It tends to lower interest rates and to permit the "fringe of unsatisfied borrowers" to get finance.

Relatively to given expectations of profit, a fall in interest rates will stimulate investment somewhat, and, by putting up the Stock Exchange value of placements, it may encourage ex-

---

[2] See "Relative Movements of Real Wages and Output," *Economic Journal* (March 1939).

penditure for consumption. These influences will increase effective demand and so increase employment.

The main determinant of the level of interest rates is the state of expectations. When bondholders have a clear view of what is the normal yield which they expect to be restored soon after any temporary change, the banking system cannot move interest rates from what they are expected to be. It is the existence of uncertainty or "two views" that makes it possible for the banks to manipulate the money market. But even when the rate of interest *can* be moved in the required direction, it may not have much effect. The dominant influence on the swings of effective demand is swings in the expectation of profits.

This is the burden of the main argument. But Keynes' ideas were not always definite, precise, and consistent. Emphasis on monetary factors varies from one part of his analysis to another. In his utopian vision of a future without wars, population growth, or major inventions, he foresaw a world in which the need for accumulation will have come to an end; both the social return and the private rate of profit on investment will have fallen very low. Provided that the rate of interest is brought down correspondingly, the euthanasia of the rentier will have removed the worst vices of capitalism (though there could still be fun in speculating on the Stock Exchange). But there may be some ultimate bottom stop to the rate of interest so that it might get stuck at too high a level and bar the entry to paradise regained. This argument certainly flatters the monetary system, not so much because of the notion that liquidity preference might ultimately check accumulation, as because of the tacit assumption that successive reductions in the rate of interest could keep accumulation going in face of a falling rate of profit. (I remember that, when I came to Chapter 17, reading the proofs of *The General Theory,* I wrote that for the first time I was finding the argument difficult to follow; Keynes replied, in effect, that he was not surprised for he found it difficult himself.)

In the main argument, which concerns immediate short-period situations, while Keynes was dethroning "monetary" theory, he yet gave money great importance, even in the title of his book, *The General Theory of Employment, Interest and Money*. This was for three reasons. First, he came to it from the *Treatise* and the *Tract*. The tradition in which he was working connected the general price level with "money" (as opposed to the "real forces" at work in Volume I of the *Principles of Economics*); he came at the problem of effective demand from that side.

Second, he was influenced by a particular historical episode in which he himself played a part. For some years after the departure of sterling from the gold standard in 1931, the exchanges were strong so that the level of domestic interest rates was insulated from competition for international reserves; in 1934 the gilt-edged rate of interest was still relatively high (by the standards of those days), the economy was still in a slump, and there was a large conversion operation falling due. Keynes, in a speech delivered as Chairman of the National Mutual, argued that interest rates were too high and ought to be reduced. Gilt-edged rose sharply; this assisted the Bank of England (if it did not persuade them) to institute a period of relatively cheap money which helped to promote a boom in house-building that was in any case under way and brought some relief to the country while the world slump had scarcely begun to lift outside.

This episode confirmed Keynes' conviction that the rate of interest is a monetary phenomenon, not bound by "real forces," and at the same time gave him, perhaps, an exaggerated impression of how much good it could do.

Third, in the orthodox system that he had to attack, the rate of interest, confused with the rate of return on investment, was the regulating mechanism which caused savings to be invested and secured equilibrium with full employment. He had to make every possible concession to this point of view in order to get a hearing. It would have been much simpler to start by assuming a constant rate of interest and a perfectly elastic supply of money. But then his whole case would have been dismissed as a misunderstanding of the orthodox position. He was obliged to accept the presumptions of his critics in order to explode them from within.

COUNTERREVOLUTION AND RESTORATION

The doctrines of the *General Theory* (though, as Keynes said, "moderately conservative") were felt to be shocking. The concessions which he made to orthodoxy about the rate of interest were used to provide a mollifying version of his system of ideas which turned it back once more into a variant of the quantity theory.

Professor (now Sir John) Hicks first stepped into the field with his *IS* and *LM* curves. Construct a diagram with the rate of interest on the vertical axis and national income on the horizontal axis. The vertical axis represents some kind of index of the level of the complex of interest rates on loans and placements of all kinds. This is a convention which Keynes himself used; he conducted a large part of his argument in terms of *the* rate of interest, though reminding the reader from time to time that this is a severe simplification of a very complex concept. The horizontal axis is labeled income. This presumably means net national income (in a closed economy) though the argument seems to require gross national product at constant prices or in wage units, or perhaps output in units of employment.

The *IS* curve slopes down to the right, indicating that output is a decreasing function of the rate of interest. A level of output corresponding to a level of *IS* implies a propensity to consume; to each level of *I,* the rate of investment per annum (net or gross?), corresponds a certain level of consumption. This is intended to be a representation of the multiplier (the relation of an *increase* in consumption brought about, presumably without time lag, by an *increase* in the rate of investment) though in the diagram it seems to mean the average relation of consumption to income. No doubt these points of definition could be cleared up, but there is a more serious difficulty. What is the meaning of making the rate of investment a function of the rate of interest?

Keynes' contention was that a *fall* in the rate of interest relatively to *given* expectations of profit would, in favorable circumstances, *increase* the rate of investment. This was rather a hazy part of his argument. Kalecki amended it to show that, with given prospects of profit, a cheapening and increased availability of finance may increase *investment plans* being made to be carried out over the immediate future. When it does so, then as plans are realized in increased expenditure on investment and the multiplier gets to work on increasing consumption, current receipts of firms rise. Assuming that their plans for the future are influenced by present experience, it follows that a further rise of investment will take place. This generates a boom which will not last because after some time the growth in the stock of productive capacity competing in the market will overtake the increase in total expenditure and so bring a fall in current profits per unit of capacity, with a consequent worsening of the expected rate of profit on further investment.

Keynes was sometimes apt to collapse the future into the present in a confusing way. His account of a boom is to say that a high rate of investment causes a fall in expected profits as the supply of productive capacity increases.[3] But one thing he could never have said is that a permanently lower level of the rate of interest would cause a permanently higher rate of investment.

---

[3] *General Theory*, p. 136.

Now consider the other curve in the diagram—*LM* slopes up to the right. Here the causation is reversed—a higher level of output causes the rate of interest to be higher. Evidently there is a hard and fast fixed quantity of money (gold or cowrie shells?) without which transactions cannot take place. Thus a higher output, requiring more money in active circulation, leaves less available to satisfy liquidity preference and so is associated with a higher rate of interest.

Here the simplification of allowing *the* interest rate to stand for the terms on which finance can be obtained proves treacherous. Are we to suppose that loans are harder to get in a boom than in a slump? One of the best known lessons of monetary history (which Keynes often repeated) is that a *fall* in activity leads to a collapse of confidence and a *rise* in interest rates, whereas, at a time of high activity, high expectations of profit affect the confidence of lenders as well as borrowers.

However, in this scheme, *LM* is an increasing function of the level of income and *IS* is a decreasing function of the rate of interest. There is one level of the rate of interest and level of income at which the curves cut. This is the equilibrium position corresponding to the given fixed amount of money. Here we have the quantity theory in its purest form. If the equilibrium level of income is below that corresponding to full employment, let the authorities increase the supply of money so as to shift *LM* to the right until it cuts *IS* at the full employment level. But now a piece of Keynes' long-run speculations is introduced. There may be a minimum level below which the rate of interest will not fall however much the supply of money is increased. If this level is above the rate of interest shown by *IS* at full employment, monetary policy alone cannot do the trick. This represents the doctrine of the liquidity trap. (If Keynes' own ideas were to be put into this diagram, it would show *IS* as the volatile element, since it depends upon expectations of profit; the case where full employment cannot be reached by monetary means would be shown by *IS* falling steeply and cutting the income axis to the left of full employment.)

The concept of the liquidity trap arises from approaching the problem of unemployment from the quantity theory. According to that theory in its simplest form, the elasticity of demand for money in terms of goods is equal to unity so that an increase in the quantity of money leads to a proportional rise in the prices of goods; but, after Keynes, the qualification was introduced that the demand for money in terms of bonds may be highly elastic, so that an increase in the quantity of money runs into hoarding and fails to raise prices. On this basis was erected a number of fantastical notions, such as the view that falling prices are good for trade, because, by raising the amount of real wealth represented by a fixed stock of money, they encourage consumption. The whole complex of ideas was somehow spliced onto a Walrasian version of neoclassical theory and used to bind up the wounds which the great slump had inflicted on laissez-faire orthodoxy.

Axel Leijonhufvud's *On Keynesian Economics and the Economics of Keynes* (Oxford University Press, 1968) is valuable because he destroys this construction by its own internal contradictions and clears away a great deal of rubbish, while remaining strictly within the framework of monetary theory.

THE CHICAGO SCHOOL

The quantity theory that was being expounded at the University of Chicago, while Keynes was wrestling with the General Theory, was much more robust and self-confident than the wishy-washy "Cambridge" version. In 1934, Simons was maintaining that the slump was due to two main causes. First, trade unions exercising monopoly power in the labor market would not let money-wage rates fall; second, "It is no exaggeration to say that the major proximate factor in the present crisis is commercial banking" [4]—the reason being that any movement in business earnings leads to an expansion or contraction of credit which drives prices up or down. The instability of PT is due to the instability of MV. The remedy that he proposed was 100 percent bank reserves, so that the government would have complete control of the supply of money. The best might be to keep M constant but there is a difficulty: "The obvious weakness of fixed quantity, as a sole rule of monetary policy, lies in the danger of sharp changes on the velocity side, for no monetary system can function effectively or survive politically in the face of extreme alternations of hoarding and dishoarding." [5] The correct rule is to maintain "the constancy of some price index, preferably an index of prices of competitively produced commodities." [6]

This noble simplicity has been a good deal sophisticated by the modern Chicagoans, led by Milton Friedman. A great part of their work consists in historical investigations of the relationship between changes in the supply of money and national income in the United States. The correlations to be explained could be set out in quantity theory terms if the equation were read right-handed. Thus we might suggest that a marked rise in the level of activity is likely to be preceded by an increase in the supply of money (if M is widely defined) or in the velocity of circulation (if M is narrowly defined) because a rise in the wage bill and in borrowing for working capital is likely to precede an increase in the value of output appearing in the statistics. Or that a fall in activity sharp enough to cause losses deprives the banks of credit-worthy borrowers and brings a contraction in

---

[4] Henry C. Simons, "A Positive Program for Laissez Faire," reprinted in *Economic Policy for a Free Society* (Chicago: Chicago University Press, 1948), p. 54.

[5] "Rules Versus Authorities in Monetary Policy," *Economic Policy for a Free Society* (Chicago: Chicago University Press, 1948), p. 164.

[6] *Ibid.*, p. 183.

their position. But the tradition of Chicago consists in reading the equation from left to right. Then the observed relations are interpreted without any hypothesis at all except *post hoc ergo propter hoc.*

There is an unearthly, mystical element in Friedman's thought.[7] The mere existence of a stock of money somehow promotes expenditure. But insofar as he offers an intelligible theory, it is made up of elements borrowed from Keynes.[8] An increase in the basis of credit, say by open-market operations, permits the banks to satisfy part of the "fringe of unsatisfied borrowers" or to offer loans on easier terms; part of additional bank lending goes to various financial intermediaries and part goes into the market for bonds. A general easing of interest rates puts up the Stock Exchange. In various ways this permits investment plans to be carried out that otherwise would have been frustrated for lack of finance, as well as encouraging purchases especially of consumer durables, both because loans are easier to get and because, with a rise in the capital value of placements, rentiers reduce their rate of saving. Thus, *other things equal,* an increase in the quantity of money promotes an increase in activity.

The difference between Friedman and Keynes is not in the analysis (insofar as it is intelligible) but in emphasis. The general implication of Friedman's doctrines is that money is very important, not as a symptom but as a cause of instability. At one time he seemed to suggest that correct control of monetary policy could stabilize the economy, but in a later pronouncement he maintained that it is too difficult for the authorities to hit off the right policy and that wrong policy exaggerates instability; therefore the best policy is just to keep the quantity of money expanding at the rate (say, 4 percent per annum) which *would*

---

[7] See *The Optimum Quantity of Money,* Chapter 1.

[8] Cf. Don Patinkin, "The Chicago Tradition, the Quantity Theory and Friedman," *Journal of Money, Credit and Banking* (February 1969).

be appropriate if the economy was expanding at that rate.[9] This is a return to Simons' ideal of a constant *M*, adapted to modern notions of growth, without any of the reservations which made him hesitate to recommend it.[10]

In both these schools, Keynes' theory of the rate of interest related to liquidity preference has been twisted, one way or the other, into a version of the quantity theory; the essence of the quantity theory is that there is a definable and recognizable quantity, *M*, the movements of which have a powerful influence upon the movements of *PT*. In short, the whole argument of both schools consists in reading the quantity equation from left to right instead of from right to left.

THE THEORY OF EMPLOYMENT

Keynes himself, of course, was not contending with the bastard progeny of his own ideas. He had to combat the old orthodoxy, which lay much deeper. Hicks confused the issue by presenting his purely monetary construction as the theory of the "classics," just as Dennis Robertson confused an analysis of "the supply and demand of loanable funds" with an argument about "the real forces of productivity and thrift." The old orthodoxy was rooted in Say's Law. "What constitutes the means of payment for commodities is simply commodities. Each person's means of paying for the productions of other people consist in those which he himself possesses." [11] Or as Marshall put it:

---

[9] Cf. pp. 75–76. Friedman, *The Optimum Quantity of Money*, p. 48.

[10] Friedman himself makes Simons out to have been a Keynesian and considers that he underestimated the importance of the quantity of money. See "The Monetary Theory and Policy of Henry Simons," *Journal of Law and Economics* (October 1967): reprinted in *The Optimum Quantity of Money*.

[11] J. S. Mill, quoted by A. Marshall, *Principles of Economics* (London: Macmillan), p. 710.

The whole of man's income is expended in the purchase of services and of commodities. It is indeed commonly said that a man spends some portion of his income and saves another. But it is a familiar economic axiom that a man purchases labour and commodities with that portion of his income which he saves just as much as he does with that which he is said to spend. He is said to spend when he seeks to obtain present enjoyment from the services and the commodities which he purchases. He is said to save when he causes the labour and the commodities which he purchases to be devoted to the production of wealth from which he expects to derive the means of enjoyment in the future.[12]

Saving makes available real resources—labor and means of production—which will be used for investment. (Marshall admitted that the mechanism breaks down when confidence fails, but his disciples in the Treasury did not follow up that line of thought.) The latter-day neoclassicals have made the basis of the old orthodoxy much clearer than it was at the time when Keynes was trying to diagnose it. In their models it is explicitly assumed that there is and has always been correct foresight, or else "capital" is malleable so that the past can be undone (without cost) and brought into equilibrium with the future; in short, they abolish time. But this is not enough to ensure full employment. They have also to assume that the wage bargain is made in terms of product; the real-wage rate finds the level at which the stock of "capital" is squeezed up or spread out to employ the available labor force. Keynes took it for granted that in an industrial economy wage rates are set in terms of general purchasing power; and he brought the argument down from the cloudy realms of timeless equilibrium to here and now, with an irrevocable past, facing an uncertain future. Money then comes into the argument as "the link between the present and the fu-

---

[12] *Pure Theory of Domestic Values* (1879), reprinted in Scarce Tract series (London: London School of Economics, 1930), p. 34.

ture." The General Theory is a "monetary theory" only in the sense that relationships and institutions concerned with money, credit, and finance are necessary elements in the "real" economy with which it is concerned.

INFLATION

Of all the conclusions of the Keynesian Revolution, the most disruptive of orthodoxy was the proposition that there is no such thing as an equilibrium of the general price level. The price level in an industrial economy is a historical accident. The main influence upon the level of prices, at any moment, is the level of money-wage rates, and the level of money-wage rates, at any moment, is the result of movements that have taken place over the distant or recent past. Prices, certainly, may move relatively to money-wage rates, over the long run with changes in productivity and over the short run with changes in the level of profit margins (the degree of monopoly), but these movements, which effect the level of real wages, are confined within narrow limits by technical and market relationships, while the level of money-wages and prices is not tethered to anything and may change (at least upward) without any limit at all.

The orthodox theory that Keynes was attacking maintained that a cut in money-wage rates means a cut in real wages and that a cut in real wages induces an increase in employment.[13] Keynes' argument was not the one which has been foisted on him by the bastard Keynesians—that money-wage rates are rigid for institutional reasons. It was that if wages could be cut, in a slump, it would make the situation worse, because it would lead to falling prices and expectations of further falls, so that investment was discouraged, while the fall in the money value of

---

[13] See The Report of the Macmillan Committee on *Finance* and *Industry*, 1931, Addendum III by T. E. Gregory.

assets would reduce the availability of credit and is liable to break the banks.[14]

There was one grain of truth in the orthodox doctrine: if one country can succeed in lowering money-wage rates relatively to those of its trade rivals, it gains a competitive advantage. This is one of the "beggar-my-neighbor remedies for unemployment." Keynes pointed out that the same advantage could be gained in much less painful manner by depreciating the exchange rate.

While Keynes was immediately concerned with the causes and consequences of a deficiency of effective demand, he also provided the basis for the analysis of inflation. In spite of his own optimism, the argument of the General Theory suggested that it would be by no means a simple matter to cure capitalism of its major defect and leave the rest of its mechanisms intact. It seemed obvious that the continuous full employment would be accompanied by a continuous fall in the value of money which might disrupt the basis of the whole system. A rise of prices, however it is caused, cannot in itself produce continuing inflation. A rise of prices of goods sold to the public reduces the expenditure in real terms of household incomes and increases the share of profit in value added. The immediate impact of the inflation exhausts itself in a change in the distribution of real income between firms and households. But this sets the stage for a change in money incomes. There are two channels for further inflation—via profits and via wages. If firms expect the favorable situation to last, they may step up plans for investment; dividends may be increased; share prices are likely to rise, causing capital gains; thus rentier incomes are increased in money terms. More immediately, the balance of power in wage-bargaining shifts to the workers' side. Firms, seeing good pros-

---

[14] See Keynes, "The Consequences for the Banks of the Collapse of Money Values" (August 1937), reprinted in *Essay in Persuasion* (London: Macmillan, 1951), p. 168 ff.

pects of profits, are reluctant to provoke strikes; in a situation of general high employment there are acute scarcities of some types of labor; the cost of living has recently risen. Money-wage rates for some groups catch up on or overtake the rise of prices, and other groups have a strong claim to match their increases. Thus rises in money incomes and expenditure increase demand and rises in wage rates increase costs. The effect of the original rise in prices is frustrated, and prices rise again.

The distinction between "demand-pull" and "cost-push" is not very useful when applied to the market for goods but it has an important meaning when applied to the market for labor. An excess demand for labor creates a situation in which firms, competing for hands, raise effective wages by various devices above the rates agreed with the trade unions. This also, of course, creates a situation favorable to increasing agreed rates. Thus demand-pull encourages cost-push. Pure cost-push is seen when there is unemployment and slack demand for labor but the trade unions are able to enforce rises in wage rates all the same.

The direction in which the vicious spiral of wages and prices is spinning may have an influence on the level of real wages. When the movement starts from prices (say, as a result of a sharp upswing in effective demand or of an increase in indirect taxes) it may be impossible for money-wages to catch up; when the movement starts from the side of wages there may be a delay in the adjustment of prices, so that there is, at least for some time, an improvement in real wages, at least for the best organized groups of workers. (One of the main difficulties of so-called incomes policy is to persuade the trade unions that they cannot benefit from raising money-wage rates, because to some extent they can.)

Keynes' argument about the relation of wages to exchange rates also takes on a new meaning in an inflationary situation. A country where money-wage rates, relative to output per head,

rise faster than in the rest of the capitalist world is liable
to develop a deficit in the balance of trade; this undermines confidence and produces a deficit in the balance of payments. A
depreciation of the currency, insofar as it is effective in redress-
ing the balance of trade, increases inflationary pressure and is
liable to wipe out the benefit by causing wages to rise all the
faster. Thus there is a second vicious spiral, of wages and exchange rates as well as of wages and prices.

The prediction that continuous inflation must sooner or later
undermine confidence in the currency and lead to hyperinflation
turns out to have been exaggerated. The system has proved
capable of adapting itself, with surprising success, to a continuously falling value of money. All the same, its consequences are
extremely demoralizing. The distribution of income thrown up
by the market economy can be tolerated as long as every individual feels that his position in it is due to fate or to his own
merits. When it becomes clear that the relative incomes of individuals are mainly determined by the bargaining position of
the group to which they belong, the ethics of the system—a fair
day's work for a fair day's wage—disintegrates, industrial dis-
cipline is undermined, and the tradition of public service gives
way to a general scramble for advantage—even doctors and
school teachers are exasperated at the erosion of their position
to the point of striking for more pay.

An incomes policy which would check inflation by preventing
overall money incomes from rising faster than overall real output would require a general acceptance of some pattern of rewards for various kinds of work. Once traditions have been
questioned, there is no acceptable criterion for deciding what it
should be. Still less is there any acceptable criterion for deciding the general distribution between work and property, especially since the old argument that the rich are necessary to society because they provide savings has been discredited. Moreover, even if it were possible to find an acceptable incomes

policy, to apply it would require a fundamental change in the traditional powers of both workers and employers which neither side is willing to accept. Perhaps the modern revival of a doctrine so unconvincing as the quantity theory of money can be explained as a refuge from the uncomfortable thought that the general level of prices has become a political problem.

Kalecki's interpretation of the General Theory was less optimistic than Keynes'. He foresaw a political trade cycle; governments would vacillate between fear of inflation and fear of unemployment; the stop-go cycle would overlay a general trend of accumulation. "The regime of the 'political business cycle' would be an artificial restoration of the position as it existed in nineteenth-century capitalism. Full employment would be reached only at the top of the boom, but slumps would be relatively mild and short lived." [15] It is now necessary to add that the system appears to grow progressively more difficult to control as time goes by. During periods of high activity prices and money incomes rise. During the slack periods they do not fall. Indeed they may continue to rise. The doctrine that a small percentage of statistical unemployment is sufficient to keep prices constant cannot hold, for as soon as it is discussed in public the trade unions hear about it and become determined to prove it false. The notion that a fall in demand lowers prices also becomes dubious. The profit margins set by the powerful firms do not correspond to the pure monopoly prices of static theory. They are set at a level calculated to yield a satisfactory return on some normal or standard average level of utilization of capacity. A fall in sales raises unit costs. The seller has no motive for lowering prices and will feel it appropriate to raise them. Thus, the political trade cycle is overlaid by a chronic tendency to rising prices. Inflation is favorable to profits, for

---

[15] "Political Aspects of Full Employment," *The Political Quarterly* (October/December 1943).

over and above the return due to "value added" by incurring costs of production there is an extra element due to the passage of time. Stocks bought at one date can be sold at a higher price merely because they are sold later. The product of labor paid at today's wage rates will live to compete with products paid for at higher wages. When investment is planned and debts incurred on the basis of expectations that inflation will continue, a check to rising prices would cause acute financial embarrassment and might precipitate a sharp slump. An inflationary economy is in the situation of a man holding a tiger by the tail.

The soothing doctrines of the bastard Keynesians have been a very poor preparation for the actual problems of modern capitalism.

THE UNIT OF ACCOUNT

Continuous inflation is a great nuisance for the governments and for a majority of the citizens of the countries where it occurs. It is also a nuisance for accountants and economists. Inflation destroys the convention that "a shilling is a shilling." The purchasing power of money has to be related to the time at which it is to be spent; the rate of profit on investment and the rate of interest are not the same in terms of money as in terms of purchasing power. The actual realized profit over a past period can be deflated by whatever seems to be the most appropriate index number, though it is never simple and obvious what index number is appropriate. This concerns the man of words who is recording past history. The man of deeds who plans investment or places his wealth on the Stock Exchange has to consider a future which is yet unknown. The expectations which guide his conduct may or may not turn out to have been well founded. All this adds great complications to an analysis which is sufficiently complicated when the purchasing power of money has an agreed objective meaning. In order to discuss old-fashioned questions we have adopted the old-fashioned convention of assuming a constant actual and expected purchasing power of money over consumption goods, so that the rate of profit on capital has the same meaning in real and in money terms. When the questions have been dealt with on this basis, it will be necessary to take them to pieces again to discuss the complications that have to be incorporated into the analysis in a world in which there is no unit of value that has an agreed and unambiguous meaning.

7

THE THEORY OF
THE FIRM

The so-called theory of the firm that was being debated before imperfect competition came into fashion[1] (and which survives in many modern textbooks) arose from the attempt to find an answer to "Marshall's dilemma."[2] If competition means that each producer can sell as much as he pleases at the going market price, then to maximize profits he goes on expanding output so long as marginal cost is less than price. But if long-period average costs fall as output expands, because of economies of scale, marginal cost is less than average cost. There is no position of long-period equilibrium until one firm has established a monopoly. To resolve this contradiction, Pigou introduced the idea of an optimum size of firm. A firm, on this view, consists of a unit of the factor of production, "management"; there are diminishing returns, after a certain point, from the application of the other factors, labor and capital, to this unit. Diseconomies of large-scale management set in, offsetting the economies of specialization. The long-period average-cost curve for

---

[1] See "Increasing Returns and the Representative Firm: A Symposium," *Economic Journal* (March 1930).

[2] Cf. above, p. 58.

the firm has a U shape; at the minimum point, in equilibrium, long-period marginal cost, long-period average cost, and the price of the commodity being produced are all equal. (The argument is simple only when the firms in one industry are producing a single homogeneous output.) The optimum size of firm relative to the market in which it is operating must be small enough to establish a sufficiently large number of firms to keep competition going.

At each moment the firm is maximizing its current profits by selling the output at which marginal short-period cost is equal to price. When price exceeds long-run average cost a supernormal profit is attracting new competition; when it is below, investment is being siphoned off into other industries. Costs include the rate of interest on finance. In equilibrium, price (and short-period marginal cost) exceeds average prime cost by a sufficient margin to permit quasirents to accrue at the level which will provide for replacement and normal profit on the investment involved at a rate equal to the ruling rate of interest.

A variant of the scheme was set out in Hicks' *Value and Capital* (a book which had an important influence in the revival of orthodoxy after Keynes). There, it is tacitly assumed that each industry consists of a fixed number of firms so that, for every commodity, the price (equal to marginal cost) is an increasing function of the level of output. In this scheme, Walrasian prices governed by supply and demand take the place of Pigovian costs of production including normal profits.

PERFECT AND IMPERFECT COMPETITION

The short-period analysis of prices in both schemes depends upon competitive conditions, not in a vague Marshallian sense, but on the strict assumptions of an indefinitely large number of independent sellers in a perfect market, which entails a perfectly elastic demand, at the ruling market price, for the product of each seller. Each firm is producing its short-period capacity output (unless it has temporarily gone out of business because the ruling price is below its average prime cost). The limit on output is set by rising marginal cost; for any greater output, marginal cost would exceed the selling price.

In the slump it was sufficiently obvious that plants were not being operated at full capacity with rising marginal costs; the upshot of the debate which broke out in the 1930s was that firms set prices by adding a gross margin to prime costs; below designed capacity, prime costs per unit of output is a constant or decreasing function of the level of output; if prime cost is identified with marginal cost, clearly it is much less than price. To reconcile this with the assumption of profit-maximizing policy, the idea was introduced that marginal revenue is related to price by the formula $e/e-1$, where e is the elasticity of demand from the point of view of the individual seller; but since this e, if it exists at all, can only be a calculation in the minds of individuals concerned with price policy, it does not add much to the argument.[3]

Even in prosperous times it is unusual for most plants to be working to capacity—if capacity were the limit to output there would be no need for advertisement. In a normal situation, it seems, there are many firms which would produce a larger output if it could be sold at the going price. Customers distribute themselves among rival sellers according to inertia, proximity, genuine differences in needs or tastes, and response to the blandishments of salesmanship. Moreover, when an acute seller's market is being enjoyed with full-capacity operation, it is prudent to allow delivery dates to lengthen rather than to choke off excess demand by high prices. Thus the system of analysis ac-

[3] For an account of my own contribution to this debate, see the Preface to the second edition of *The Economics of Imperfect Competition* (London: Macmillan, 1969).

cording to which price equals marginal cost, so that the level of gross profits is governed by the excess of marginal cost over average-price cost, is seen to be without application.

With this, the notion of wages equal to value of marginal product also collapses. When a plant is being worked below designed capacity with constant average prime costs, a loss of one man-shift of work entails a loss of the average value of output of one man.

In general in modern industry, it seems that the wage bill is about half of value added. In the typical case, then, the value of marginal product of labor is twice the wage. Hicks was quite correct in saying that to abandon the assumption of perfect competition "must have very destructive consequences for economic theory" if economic theory means nothing more than Walrasian general equilibrium.[4]

The long-period aspect of the Pigovian scheme is even less convincing. The individual firm is not supposed to be aiming at the optimum size. It is aiming at maximizing the flow of net profit to be got in any situation. Then whenever a firm finds itself with a rate of profit in excess of the rate of interest, it surely must be carrying out investment in order to get more profit in the future. The argument is concerned with a stationary state, with fixed "resources"; it is intended to show how given resources are allocated between different uses; a constant total of "capital" is washing about between different industries finding the level at which the rate of profit is equalized. But once profit-maximizing firms are allowed into the story, how can accumulation be kept out?

The essence of the competitive process is that some firms take business away from others. Those which are successful grow faster than industry as a whole, those which are least successful

---

[4] See *Value and Capital,* p. 83 (Oxford: Clarendon Press, 1939).

cease to exist. Pigou's concept of managerial diseconomies of scale, perhaps, can be applied to the kind of business where "the entrepreneur" is a particular individual. As a business grows beyond the scope of one-man management it runs into difficulties.[5] But this is an exceptional case. At any moment there may be a number of individuals who have found a satisfactory niche and manage to maintain independence, but the majority of businesses are either growing, being forced out of existence by the growth of others, or being absorbed into some larger organization.

Why do firms grow? Some contemporary writers are inclined to treat growth as a specially modern phenomenon arising from the divorce between control and property in the modern corporation, legally owned by a floating population of shareholders and operated by a cadre of salaried managers; they seem to suggest that there was a past period to which the textbook scheme applied. Yet obviously the successful family businesses of the early nineteenth century must have been just as keen on growth as any modern corporation. Anyone who is in business naturally wants the business to survive (particularly if his own heirs and successors are involved) and to survive it is necessary to grow. When a business is prosperous it is making profits; for that very reason it is threatened with competition; it would be feckless to distribute the whole net profit to the family for consumption; part must be ploughed back in increasing capacity so as to supply a growing market, to prevent others coming in, or to diversify production if the original market is not expanding. Any one, by growing, is threatening the position of others, who retaliate by expanding their own capacity, reducing production costs, changing the design of commodities, or introducing new devices of salesmanship. Thus each has to run to keep up with the rest.

---

[5] See E. A. G. Robinson, *The Structure of Competitive Industry*, *Cambridge Handbook* (London: Nisbet, 1931).

As we have seen, the very fact that investment is going on is generating opportunities for profitable sales,[6] so that as long as growth goes on, it can go on. The determination of firms to grow by reinvesting profits was characteristic of capitalism from the start; indeed, if it were not the case, capitalism would never have happened.

MONOPOLY AND OLIGOPOLY

The way out of Marshall's dilemma is in the opposite direction. Where competition is vigorous, there must be a tendency toward monopoly, which is often held up at the stage of oligopoly when a few powerful firms prefer armed neutrality to the final battle for supremacy.

Marshall accounted for growth by economies of scale [7] which give a firm a competitive advantage by reducing costs of production. This is of importance where technology demands large indivisible investments but in general the advantage to a firm of size is mainly in size itself—that is, in financial power. In Marshall's day, a particular business operated in a particular industry in which it had the technical know-how and the market connections required. Now the large corporation can jump from one industry to another, employing its own experts or buying up a smaller concern already established there. The modern development of conglomerates provides clear evidence that it is financial power, rather than technical economies of scale, that permits firms to continue to grow when they are already large.

While the reduction in the number of independent firms gen-

---

[6] See above, p. 46.

[7] In Marshall both internal and external economies accrue to the individual firm. As usual with him, the concepts are not clear-cut. Pigou distinguished between economies of scale to the firm and economies of scale to the "industry" producing a particular commodity. This is a logical set of concepts which it is not easy to apply in reality.

erates monopoly in particular industries in particular countries, the breakdown in the barriers between industries and between national economies increases competitiveness. In the textbook theory of the firm, a monopolist, faced by a known and stationary demand-curve for the commodity that he controls, restricts output to the level at which marginal revenue is equal to marginal cost and so extracts the maximum possible profit from the market. There are, certainly, examples of monopolies which conform more or less to the textbook pattern, but in general the great firms are far from restricting output—they are continuously expanding capacity, conquering new markets, producing new commodities, and exploiting new techniques. The level of profit margins and the rate of profit on investment that they enjoy are in general higher than those in stagnant markets where competition still prevails, because in expanding markets they can catch the profits that they need to finance expansion. Modern industry is a system not so much of monopolistic competition as of competitive monopolies.

The command of finance by the great firms gives them freedom to follow their own devices, manipulating not only the market economy but also national and international policy. ("What's good for General Motors is good for the United States.") The breach which this makes in the textbook scheme is much more serious than the abandonment of the doctrine that prices are governed by marginal costs which followed from the recognition of imperfect competition. It destroys the basis of the doctrine that the pursuit of profit allocates resources between alternative uses to the benefit of society as a whole.

CHOICE OF TECHNIQUE

It is an absurd, though unfortunately common, error to suppose that substitution between labor and capital is exhibited by a movement from one point to another along a pseudoproduction function.[8] Each point represents a situation in which prices and wages have been expected, over a long past, to be what they are today, so that all investments have been made in the form that promises to yield the maximum net return to the investor. The effect of a change in factor prices cannot be discussed in these terms. Time, so to say, runs at right angles to the page at each point on the curve. To move from one point to another we would have either to rewrite past history or to embark upon a long future. In dynamic conditions, changes in the composition of demand, changes in technique, and changes in costs of specific factors of production are continuously going on. Investments are always made in less than perfect knowledge of present possibilities and less than perfect confidence in expectations about the future. The stock of capital in existence today is not that which would have been chosen if the future, that is now today, had been correctly foreseen in the past. It is not composed of units of the most appropriate technique; it contains numerous fossils from earlier periods of techniques which were chosen in conditions different from those obtaining today. Nor is it ever being maintained in a constant form. It is continually being done over as gross investment replaces one set of capital goods by another set appropriate to a new complex of expectations. To discuss the choice of technique, we must look, not at the total stock of capital as at a point on pseudo-production function, but at the investment plans which are being made at each moment.

In the Pigovian scheme any firm can borrow as much or as little as it pleases at the ruling rate of interest. In an equilibrium position, no firm is planning to make any net investment, for if it expanded its productive capacity, managerial diseconomies would cause average costs to rise and the additional returns from

---

[8] E.g., R. M. Solow, "On the Rate of Return: Reply to Pasinetti," *Economic Journal* (June 1970).

an increment of output would not be enough to cover the increment on the interest bill for the additional finance. The technique of production that it has chosen is controlled by the rate of interest and the level of wages, according to the rule that a given output is produced at minimum cost. In a dynamic economy the rate of interest may, perhaps, be supposed to have some influence on the amount of investment which is being planned at any moment,[9] but there is no reason why it should influence the choice of technique. With the finance that it is planning to invest, the firm must be supposed to prefer a plan promising a greater increment of profit to one promising less, irrespective of what it had to pay for the finance.[10] But the problem of choosing between plans is indefinitely complicated; decisions may actually be made on hunch or on some conventional rule such as a pay-off period.[11] When sophisticated estimates are made of discounted cash flow, it is the expected rate of profit that comes into the calculation, not the rate of interest. There is an important way, however, that the distribution of available finance between firms affects the techniques that are adopted—that is, when the minimum size of an efficient installation is very large. Then only a powerful firm can attempt it. Smaller firms have to be content with less ambitious projects. The powerful firm undertakes such an investment only when it has sufficient control over the market to be confident of a satisfactory return,[12] while the small-scale competitive producers have to be satisfied with a lower rate.

---

[9] Cf. above, p. 31.

[10] Cf. M. Kalecki, *Essays in the Theory of Economic Fluctuations* (London: Allen & Unwin, 1939).

[11] N. Kaldor and J. A. Mirrlees, "A New Model of Economic Growth," *Review of Economic Studies* (June 1962).

[12] This point was forcefully made by Schumpeter. See *Capitalism, Socialism and Democracy* (New York: Harper, 1942), Chapter 8. See also J. K. Galbraith, *The New Industrial State* (New York: Houghton Mifflin, 1967), Chapter 19.

The most important influence upon the choice of technique is not the cost of finance or "factor prices" but the rate of investment relative to the availability of labor. When, as may happen in the early stages of industrialization, an individual firm can employ as much labor as it likes at a constant wage rate, it may be supposed to find the technique that promises the highest return per unit of investment and carry on its expansion by gradually increasing employment with the same type of equipment. If a new technique is offered which is superior to that in use, in the sense that at current prices it both reduces the cost of investment per man and reduces the wage bill per unit of output, then a keen profit-maximizer will install it, but there is no great compulsion to do so.

The situation is very different in an environment of near-full employment. A large firm whose plants provide an appreciable proportion of the jobs in particular regions has to consider, when planning investment, how much more labor it will be able to recruit. It will generally find it necessary to carry out expansion, at least partly, by raising investment per man employed. It is not provided with a predigested "book of blueprints" of techniques; it must find out what the possibilities are and assess them as best it may. Nor is there any reason to suppose that the process necessarily involves "capital deepening" and a fall in the rate of profit. In the course of exploring ways of raising output per head it will often succeed in developing superior techniques. The successful firms have no great objection to allowing money-wage rates to rise; they may even be bidding for labor by offering various inducements to attract men from other employers. Small firms using labor-intensive techniques must then mechanize or go out of business. Those which survive may well find themselves more prosperous in the end. Since, as output per head rises, prices are likely to rise less than in proportion to wage rates, it is possible to see long spells of accumulation in which real-wage rates are rising but the rate of profit is not falling. In this sense, "substitution of capital for labor" is the essence of industrial development, but it has nothing whatever to do with the factor prices shown on a pseudoproduction function.

MACRO AND MICRO THEORY

There have been many accounts of the behavior of particular firms (investigations connected with antimonopoly legislation in various countries are a rich source) and statistical inquiries into the behavior of gross margins, the profitability of different types of organization, and so forth. This has mainly been pure description without benefit of theory or it has befuddled itself with attempts to fit into an inappropriate analytical scheme. A theory of the firm appropriate to a dynamic economy is in its infancy.[13]

Meanwhile, it is necessary to develop a general theory of accumulation within which a micro theory can be elaborated. At the first stage, a firm can be simply identified with the capital that it controls; the size and number of firms making up the whole industrial structure are not important in themselves. The interaction between firms, however, is important as a determinant

---

13 A "new wave" was started twelve years ago by Edith Penrose with *The Theory of the Growth of the Firm* (Oxford: Blackwell, 1959), which has been followed up by W. Baumol, *Business Behavior, Value and Growth* (New York: Harcourt, Brace & Jovanovich), R. Marris, *Managerial Capitalism* (London: Macmillan, 1964), M. Gordon, *The Investment, Financing and Valuation of the Corporation* (Homewood, Ill.: Richard D. Irwin, 1964), and many others. In each of their models the policy of the firm is to aim at growth, restrained by a diversity of limitations. Any simple formula to describe the motivation of firms is unlikely to be satisfactory because their behavior is highly complex and various. The neo-neoclassical hypothesis that the aim of a firm is to maximize the present value of its shares does not seem to say anything very precise, for the main influence on the present value of shares is the expectations which the market holds about the future growth of their value.

of accumulation and technical progress in industry as a whole. The behavior of a particular firm may be discussed in terms of its reaction to prospective profits, but accumulation cannot be explained in terms of prospects of profit which have an objective basis apart from the investment that is induced by them. When firms are cautious and reluctant to invest except for a high rate of return, the return that they actually get will be low, because sluggish investment and high-profit margins restrict effective demand. The prospect of profit for each depends on what the rest are doing.

In any case, accumulation cannot be accounted for only by the prospect of profits. If investors were solely concerned to find the best return on the finance that they command, the less successful firms would stop investing and place their funds by buying shares of the more successful. As Keynes remarked, "Enterprise only pretends to itself to be mainly actuated by its own prospectus, however candid and sincere." [14] The state of the "animal spirits," which is largely a function of the energy and competitiveness of groups of firms, is the most important factor in capitalist development, though it by no means follows that the most energetic enterprise necessarily produces the most beneficial results for society as a whole.

----

[14] *General Theory,* p. 160.

8

GROWTH
MODELS
For the classical economists, economic growth brought about by
capital accumulation and technical progress was the central
problem; in the neoclassical era it was little discussed, except
vaguely by Marshall, who retained something of the tradition of
Ricardo; after the Keynesian Revolution it came back into fashion.

The treatment of growth in von Neumann's ultraclassical
model is brutally simple. A technically specified wage is the cost
of labor and bodies are becoming available to carry it out at the
rate at which the output of wage goods is growing. The first
long-run Keynesian model was proposed by Harrod. For him,
the "natural" rate of growth of the effective supply of labor is
given exogenously and the rate of growth of the economy may
or may not keep up with it. In the neo-neoclassical models that
have since proliferated, the natural rate of growth is automatically realized by some kind of equilibrating mechanism.

HARROD

The great strength of Harrod's model is that it is not an equilibrium scheme. It is a projection into the long-period of the concepts of the General Theory. Accumulation comes about through

109

decisions taken by profit-seeking firms and there is no guarantee that the rate of investment in uncontrolled private enterprise will be either steady or at a desirable level. Unfortunately, his own exposition of his model [1] is almost as confusing as the interpretations that neo-neoclassicals have put upon it.

The share of net saving in net income, s, is determined by the propensity to save the public; the capital to output ratio, v, is given by technical conditions. Therefore there is only one possible maintainable growth rate, $g = s/v$. This is the "warranted" rate of growth. It is important to realize that this does not mean the rate of growth that firms will actually undertake or the rate that they decide or desire to carry out in the given conditions. It is the rate that they would have to carry out in order to be satisfied, after the event, with what they have done, so as to be willing to continue. The warranted rate of growth is an expression of the thriftiness conditions of the economy. A high warranted rate of growth (relatively to the desire of firms to accumulate) generates underconsumption and so reduces actual growth. A low warranted rate generates inflationary conditions and stimulates growth.

The concept of s and v being exogenously determined gives rise to the problem that has become known as Harrod's knife-edge, though Sir Roy himself repudiates it. In long-period terms: the formula, $g = s/v$, is equivalent to $I/K = I/Y \cdot Y/K$, the ratio of net investment to the stock of capital is equal to the share of net investment in net income multiplied by the capital to income ratio, all in value terms. (The money prices of consumer goods are assumed constant, so that values can be expressed in money.) The formula grew out of a trade-cycle theory

---

[1] See "An Essay in Dynamic Theory," *Economic Journal* (March 1939): *Towards a Dynamic Economy* (London: Macmillan, 1949), and "A Comment on Joan Robinson's 'Harrod After Twenty One Years,'" *Economic Journal* (September 1970).

and Sir Roy seems reluctant to admit that *net* income and in-vestment have a precise value only in conditions of steady growth or that the meaning of v that satisfies the formula $v = s/g$ is the value of capital over the value of net income. For him v seems to mean the incremental capital to output ratio somehow expressed in physical terms.

The main mechanism in the trade-cycle theory was of the "capital-stock-adjustment" type but it can equally well be inter-preted in terms of expectations of profit. In any given situation, with given physical productive capacity, an *increase* in the rate of gross investment raises the level of current gross profits above what it was in the immediate past. If the improvement in pros-pects is expected to last, investment will increase further and so profits will rise further; in short, a boom develops. Contrariwise when the rate of investment falls. This part of the argument is concerned with assumptions about the actual behavior of an actual economy. The "warranted rate of growth" is a meta-physical concept. It concerns the *existence* of a possible equilib-rium path, not the stability of any path that an economy may be following. The problem of the knife-edge is the problem of the one and only possible value of g compatible with exogenously given values of s and v.

Taking the Harrod formula out of Sir Roy's hands, we can attempt to find out the meaning of the assumptions which it requires.

The neo-neoclassicals seized upon Harrod's model and thrust it into a pre-Keynesian mould.[2] The rate of saving governs the rate of investment. The "warranted rate of growth" is realized, whatever it may be. When $v < s/n$, there is more saving than is

---

[2] See, in particular, Trevor W. Swan, "Growth Models: of Golden Ages and Production Functions" in *Economic Development*, ed. K. Ber-rill (London: Macmillan, 1964). International Economic Association Conference at Camagori.

needed to look after *n,* the natural rate of growth (presumably the argument always starts from a position of full employment); *g* then exceeds *n.* There is a well-behaved production function in output, labor, and "capital." Excess saving is raising the "capital" to labor ratio, the rate of profit is falling, and the real-wage rate rising. As *v* rises, the amount of saving required to look after growth at the natural rate is increasing; the rate at which "deepening" is going on is decelerating, until equilibrium is reached with $g = n = s/v$. This is nothing more than the Wicksell process, in a one-commodity world,[3] superimposed upon long-run steady growth. (The story is also told backwards. When $v > s/n$, decumulation sets in, with $g < n$ and *v* falling, until the equilibrium value of *v* is established.)

To retain the Keynesian character of the growth model, we must interpret it in a different way. We must introduce another term into the argument: the rate of accumulation that firms, taken together, are willing to bring about. Harrod's central proposition is that when the firms cannot carry out accumulation at the warranted rate (for instance, because $s/v > n$) or when they are too slack to do so, underconsumption and slumpy conditions prevail, so that there is stagnation or decline over the long run (though occasional short-lived booms may occur). Thus a high value of *s,* for Harrod, plays just the opposite of its neoclassical role. For him, far from promoting a high rate of growth, it is an impediment to any growth at all.

To understand this paradox, we must examine the meanings of *g, v,* and *s* in more detail.

One of the most useful and important innovations in the Harrod scheme is the treatment of technical progress, but since the analysis is complicated we shall attempt to deal with one layer at a time. At this stage we assume that the "natural" rate of

---

[3] Cf. above, p. 70.

growth, *n,* is given only by the rate of increase of the labor force.

To strip the model to its essentials we postulate:

$$Y \equiv C + I \equiv W + P$$

that is, net income per annum is exhaustively divided into consumption and net industrial investment per annum and it is exhaustively divided into wages and profits. (Wages are taken to include all "earned income" except the high salaries of business executives, which should be included in the profits of their firms.) *K* is the value of the capital stock. The growth rate, *g,* is *I/K;* this entails that the capital to income ratio, *v* or *K/Y,* is constant through time. The rate of profit, π, is *P/K*. At any point on a path of steady growth that is actually being realized, the initial conditions, including the physical composition of the stock of equipment, must be compatible with the growth rate that is going on. The rate of profit on capital and the share of wages and profit in net income are constant through time; the question which we have to consider is how they are related to *g, v,* and *s.*

The value of capital per man employed depends primarily upon technical conditions and upon the rate of profit. There may be a pseudoproduction function showing other possibilities, but it would not come into the story, for the technique appropriate to the growth rate and the rate of profit has already been installed at any given point on the growth path, and is being expanded with each item in proportion.

The assumption of a uniform rate of profit implies that the model is competitive in the long-period sense—no firm can make a monopolistic supernormal profit by restricting entry into its market. There is no need to assume perfect competition in the short-period sense that all plant is always operated at capacity with sharply rising marginal costs, so that gross profit margins are determined by marginal cost minus average prime cost,

fluctuating with every seasonal or random change in demand.
We may assume that firms set prices by a mark-up on prime cost
in such a way that, if *normal* capacity operation is realized on
the average, receipts will cover total cost including amortization
and yield a net profit per annum that corresponds to the rate of
profit that they hope to enjoy. (Over a period when average
utilization exceeds the normal level, actual net profit exceeds expectations, and contrariwise. On our tranquil path, we may
suppose that normal utilization is realized on the average, though
not necessarily without variations week by week.)

The degree of monopoly, or ratio of gross margins to prime
cost, now comes into the determination of v, the capital to income ratio. The length of the standard working day, the preva-
lence of multiple shifts and so forth are subsumed under the
given long-period technical conditions, but the degree of utilization of plant is connected with the short-period price-policy of
firms. (We must suppose that working hours may vary with
overtime or that the normal level of employment is less than 100
percent of available labor.) With given plant, a higher degree of
monopoly means a lower ratio of normal to full-capacity operation and therefore a higher cost of investment per unit of output.

So much for v; we must now consider s. On what assumptions
could we find s, the share of net saving in net income, to be given
independently of the rate of profit on capital and the share of
profit in net income? (Sir Roy discusses the influence of the rate
of interest received by rentiers on the subjective desire to save
but he neglects the effect of the distribution of income between
wages and profits.) We are not obliged to assume that every
family saves the same proportion, s, of its income. There may be
different proportions of saving by rich and poor, provided that
the distribution of income between families remains constant
through time, but poverty and wealth must not be correlated
with earned and unearned income. Rentier property—bonds,
share, and cash—must be randomly distributed through the

population so that the representative family is drawing income from wages and from interest and is saving a certain proportion of its total income from both sources. (There must be a banking system which keeps the quantity of money growing at the right rate to provide for the growing wage bill and for any holdings of cash due to liquidity preference, so as to keep the rate of interest constant through time at a level compatible with the rate of accumulation that is going on.) The firms retain enough gross profit to keep capital intact (in physical and in value terms). We may suppose either that net profit is fully distributed to shareholders and finance for net investment raised by means of new issues of shares and bonds; or we may suppose that rentier income includes capital gains due to investment of retained profits and that the saving ratio, *s,* covers this part of income as well as the rest. In such a world, the firms (taken together) are free to make the level of prices and the rate of profit what they please by the level at which they set gross margins. Let us suppose money-wage rates are fixed once and for all. Comparing a higher with a lower degree of monopoly, the prices of consumer goods are higher and the prices of investment goods are adjusted accordingly. With a given level of employment, the wage bill is the same in the two positions; where prices are higher gross profits are higher. (When Δp is the excess of prices and G is gross profits, $\Delta G = \frac{\Delta p}{p}(G + W)$.) The extra gross profit is being paid out for replacements in the investment sector and as income to households. The higher prices reduce the purchasing power of wages but the increment of rentier income exactly compensates. The volume of outlay for consumption is higher by the same amount as the value of goods sold at the prices fixed by the firms; sY, net saving in money terms, is higher by the same amount as I, net investment; A, amortization allowances in money terms are higher by the same amount as D, outlay for maintenance of stock of physical capital.

We now see the force of the expression "the degree of monopoly." Provided that, when the price leader in each market sets a certain level of gross margins on his own prime costs all sellers abide by the corresponding prices, each getting a margin which depends on his own costs, then the price leader can set prices as he pleases. But there is always a danger that some cad, not content with his share, will try to increase his sales by undercutting, and margins will come tumbling down. The freedom of a price leader is limited by the dispersion of costs and the aggressiveness of potential competitors. Thus, in a general broad sense, the less competitive is the general situation in an economy, the higher the "degree of monopoly," measured by the ratio of gross margins to prime cost, is likely to be.

Now consider the formula, $g = s/v$. The rate of profit may be supposed to have an influence upon v, the capital to income ratio, but this cannot be relied upon to get us off the knife-edge. Given s and g, there is only one value of v compatible with equilibrium. With a single technique, v may vary over a certain range with the rate of profit (the value of a given stock of equipment in terms of output rises or falls with the rate of profit according to the time-pattern of production); on the pseudo-production function there may be no rate of profit that yields the required value of v (allowing for utilization) or there may be several. (This was established in the "reswitching" debate.) Even if there is a convenient value of v, corresponding to one rate of profit, there is no mechanism in the system to bring it into being. There is no way in which a rate of profit determined by short-period price-policy can be supposed to find the value that, if it obtained in long-period conditions, would be compatible with the right value of v.

Evidently the knife-edge is a chimera. The problem is created by the unnatural assumption that s, the ratio of net saving to net income, is determined by the psychology of households rather than by the requirements of firms. All the same, in exploring it we have learned something of value.

PROFITS AND SAVING

The problem of the knife-edge disappears when we recognize that profits provide the main source of saving and that investment generates the profits that it needs. The principal source of finance for gross investment is retention of gross profits by firms. (Expenditure on investment precedes the receipt of the profits to which it gives rise; in a growing economy firms must be borrowing from banks the difference between this month's outlay and the receipts of, say, six months ago.) [4] When investment exceeds retentions, there is saving by households. (In our simplified model there is no excess of saving over the investment carried out by firms—no private house-building, budget deficit, or balance of trade—so that household income exceeds consumption only by the excess of investment over retention of profits by firms.) [5] Household savings are borrowed by the firms to finance the excess of investment over their own retentions, directly by sales of securities, or indirectly through the banking system, which is providing deposits to satisfy the liquidity preference of rentiers, over and above their short-term lending to firms.

In our model, the issue of equities is treated simply as a form of borrowing and rentiers are regarded as treating shares simply as income-yielding placements, not as a controlling interest in firms. The relation between borrowing by issuing shares and on bonds of various kinds is a very intricate subject (complicated by the legal fiction that interest is a cost but dividends are not). Here we have all this on one side and postulate that the only form of long-term borrowing is the issue of shares.[6]

---

[4] Cf. p. 74 above.

[5] Income of households is here exclusive of capital gains. See below, p. 120, note 12.

[6] We must therefore suppose that when banks provide deposits to satisfy the liquidity preference of rentiers, they hold shares of firms.

In the simple case where there is no saving out of wages, the rate of profit on a steady growth path is given by the formula $\pi = g/s_p$—the level of net profits is such as to provide net saving per annum equal to net investment. Then, whatever $gv/$ may be, s is equal to it, for the share of profit adjusts in such a way as to make it so.[7] Provided that the firms are willing to carry out investment at such a level as to make $g = n$, that is, to realize the natural rate of growth; and provided that it is physically possible for them to do so—the initial conditions at any moment are appropriate; and politically possible—the real-wage rate, governed by technical conditions and the rate of profit given by $\pi = g/s_p$, is not below the tolerable level, then growth at the natural rate takes place. But even if all the other conditions are fulfilled, growth at the natural rate will not be realized if firms lack the energy to carry it out. There is no law of nature that the "natural" rate of growth should prevail. This marks the distinction between a Keynesian and a neo-neoclassical growth model.

We must now consider the relation between the degree of monopoly and the rate of profit. When there is no saving out of earned income, the rate of profit is independent of the degree of monopoly, but the real-wage rate is not. By setting higher prices (given money-wage rates) the firms can increase the profit that would be obtained from a *given* volume of sales to

---

This is forced upon us by our simplifying assumptions which exclude bonds and government debt. But equally in a more realistic case, when the quantity of money is increased to provide a placement for household saving, the banks must be acquiring assets which the savers do not fancy.

[7] Keynes simplified his model the other way. In the main part of the argument of the *General Theory* liquidity preference is presented as a choice between bonds and money. There are allusions to the yield of shares as a rate of interest, but they are not fully worked out. However, in the *Treatise* the main argument is conducted in terms of equities.

the public but they cannot ensure that the volume of expenditure by the public will increase accordingly. Even if additional profits were paid out to rentiers instantaneously, the firms would get back only $(1 - s_p) \Delta P$ of expenditure from every increase in P. Thus the rate of profit, $\pi = g/s_p$, is independent of the degree of monopoly. A higher level of prices, however, reduces the real wage; the wage rate corresponding to a given value of π is not independent of the degree of monopoly. (With a given level of employment, a higher degree of monopoly entails a lower level of utilization of plant and a higher value of K/Y. Therefore, with a given rate of profit it entails a higher share of profit in income and a lower real wage per man employed.) [8]

We must now introduce saving out of earned income. Luigi Pasinetti proposed a neat model in which the rate of profit is equal to the rate of growth divided by capitalists' saving even when there is some saving out of wages.[9] He divided the economy into two classes, capitalists and worker-rentiers who earn wages and receive profits on their accumulated savings; and he assumed that the rate of profit is the same on capital owned by both classes.[10] We can elaborate on the argument by making some

---

[8] This is the long-period version of Kalecki's famous theory: the workers spend what they get and the capitalists get what they spend. When there is no saving out of wages, gross profit, over any period, is equal to gross investment plus capitalists' consumption; and the share of wages in proceeds is the inverse of the degree of monopoly. See *Essays in the Theory of Economic Fluctuations* (London: Allen & Unwin, 1938), p. 76.

[9] See "The Rate of Profit and Income Distribution in Relation to the Rate of Economic Growth," *Review of Economic Studies* (October 1967).

[10] His critics pointed out that if the share of wages in net income is sufficiently high it is possible for the proportion of total net saving provided by the worker-rentiers to exceed that provided by capitalists even though the propensity to save of the latter is higher. In such a case, the worker-rentiers are acquiring capital faster than the capitalists so that no

further distinctions. Firms are obliged to retain at least enough of gross profit to keep capital intact and they normally retain a large proportion of net profit as well. Households may be divided into three classes: rentiers who derive their whole income from placements; worker-rentiers with mixed incomes, and workers whose whole income is derived from wages. (Wages include all earned income.) [11]

We may assume that equities are held mainly by wealthy rentiers. It is now convenient to include capital gains due to investment of retained profits in the income of shareholders.[12] Taken together, the rentiers have a higher than average propensity to save, though there may be individuals among them who are dissipating wealth inherited from the past.

The worker-rentiers are mainly concerned with saving-up to spend later (through pension contributions, etc.) so that ratio of net saving to total income for this class is relatively small. They may be supposed to have a higher liquidity preference than

---

equilibrium is possible until the capitalists have ceased to own an appreciable proportion of the stock of capital; the whole net income then accrues to worker-rentiers and their propensity to save governs the share of saving in income, the *s* of Harrod's formula. Having got themselves back on to Harrod's knife-edge, the critics claim that the marginal productivity theory of distribution then becomes true. See J. E. Meade and F. H. Hahn, "The Rate of Profit in a Growing Economy," *Economic Journal* (June 1965), J. E. Meade, "The Outcome of a Pasinetti Process" (A Note), *Economic Journal* (March 1966), and P. A. Samuelson and F. Modigliani, "The Pasinetti Paradox in Neo-classical and More General Studies," *Review of Economic Studies* (October 1966).

[11] See Pasinetti, p. 113.

[12] This is a matter of accounting conventions. When retentions are treated as saving, rentier income is treated as consisting only of what is paid out to them by firms. A sale of securities to finance consumption is then treated as dis-saving. When capital gains are included in rentier income, retentions are excluded from saving, and unrealized capital gains are included in it. The share of saving in profits, s_p, is not affected by the way the accounts are set up, but it is affected by the actual behavior of rentiers.

the wealthy rentiers so that the income on their placements is much less than the rate of profit. The workers who own no property provide no net saving. Each class (taken as a whole) may be supposed to have its own propensity to save; the mixed-income class applies their propensity to save to income without distinguishing its source. The share of saving out of wages as a whole depends upon how much of the total wage bill goes into these incomes and how much to workers whose propensity to save is zero. Similarly for profits. On a steady growth path the distribution of income between classes remains constant. We can therefore regroup incomes according to their origin and postulate that s_p, the share of saving in net profit, is considerably greater than s_w, the share of saving in wages.[13]

Saving out of wages tends to reduce the rate of profit. The formula now becomes $\pi = \dfrac{g - s_w \left(\dfrac{W}{K} \right)}{s_p}$. On the other hand, saving out of wages gives some leverage to allow the degree of monopoly to affect the rate of profit. A higher level of prices relatively to money wages (with a given rate of growth being maintained) entails lower real wages; consequently less saving out wages. Profits must therefore be higher by a sufficient amount to allow saving out of profits to make up the deficiency. When real wages are less by $-\Delta W$, saving out of profits is higher by an amount equal to $s_w \Delta W$. Therefore, $\Delta P = \dfrac{s_w}{s_p} \Delta W$.

As we have already seen, when $s_w = s_p$ (Harrod's s), $\Delta P = -\Delta W$. When $s_w = 0$, $(\pi = g/s_p)$, $\Delta P = 0$. So long as $s_w < s_p$, ΔP is less than $-\Delta W$. The effect of the degree of monopoly

---

[13] In the "anti-Pasinetti" case, where the workers are acquiring a growing share of total capital, steady growth is not possible; the overall propensity to save (Harrod's s) is falling as time goes by and the rate of profit rising. It is hard to understand how this is supposed to provide support for neoclassical theory. See Pasinetti, p. 119, note 10.

upon the rate of profit is greater the smaller the difference between s_w and s_p.[14]

There is one more aspect of household savings that must be considered. The excess of investment over retentions of profits and borrowing from banks is borrowed from households. But firms are under no obligation to borrow just because households have savings that they want to place in securities. If all investment were financed by retentions there could be no *net* saving out of the incomes paid out to households as wages and dividends. Yet every household is free to save as it pleases.

Kaldor has suggested a mechanism which reconciles this apparent contradiction.[15] In a simplified form his argument is as follows. Divide all rentiers into old shareholders and new savers. The income of shareholders consists of dividends and capital gains. Net investment financed by retentions causes the value of shares to rise. In tranquil conditions, with a constant rate of interest and rate of profit, there is a constant valuation ratio, v, the ratio of the stock-exchange value of the equity of a company, V, to the value of its earning assets, K. (This must not be confused with Harrod's V, the capital to income ratio). For the typical company, which is growing at the growth rate per annum of the economy, $g = \dfrac{\Delta K}{K} = \dfrac{\Delta V}{V}$ but ΔK, the annual net investment of the firm is equal to ΔV, the annual increment of value of its outstanding shares, only when the valuation ratio is equal to one. If there are no new issues, ΔV accrues to the existing shareholders as capital gains. When part of ΔK is financed by new issues, capital gains are less than ΔV. The shareholders of the typical company (whose rate of profit is π and rate of growth

---

[14] I am indebted to Dr. Amit Bhaduri for some discussions of this point.

[15] "A Neo-Pasinetti Theorem," *Review of Economic Studies* (October 1966).

g) get the benefit of profits some time after they have accrued to the firm. When *P* is the net profit of, say, last year, and *r* is the retention ratio of that firm, the shareholders receive $(l - r)$ *P* as dividends, this year, and *rPv* as capital gains. As a continuous income per unit of capital of the firm, they receive $(l - r)$ π + *r* π *v*.

If there were an excess of positive new household saving coming onto the market for placements over the supply of new securities generated by the borrowing of firms, the valuation ratio would be driven up. A higher valuation ratio means a higher annual income for shareholders corresponding to a given rate of profit. Equilibrium is established when the expenditure for consumption of old shareholders exceeds their receipts of dividends sufficiently to require a sale of securities (realization of capital gains) that offsets the excess demand for securities coming from the new savers. The banking system is assumed to be generating a sufficient increase in the quantity of money to offset liquidity preference at the rate of interest at which net saving out of incomes paid to households, taken as a whole, is equal to net borrowing by firms. On this view, new issues by firms tend to keep up the rate of interest and to keep down the rate of profit.[16] (This very recent argument cannot strictly be regarded as an old-fashioned question, but it is necessary to complete the construction of a Keynesian growth model.)

The purpose of a growth model of this type is not to predict equilibrium but to map out the possible causes of disturbances. The assumptions of our model are too simple for testable hypotheses to be drawn from it at this stage, but it suggests some interesting lines of thought.

For instance, we have seen that in some circumstances a

---

[16] Kaldor offers the formula $\pi = (g - u)/r$ where *u* is the proportion of investment financed by new issues.

higher degree of monopoly may generate a higher rate of profit with a constant rate of growth. This does not mean that a *rise* in profit margins (with a constant rate of investment) necessarily increases profits. In any given week, the volume of expenditure for consumption goods depends upon the level of money incomes of the recent past. A rise of prices this week reduces the volume of sales and may cause unemployment. But in a modern capitalist economy where the government is concerned to maintain effective demand, the reduction of employment is offset, one way or another, by additional expenditure. Then the firms, by mutual consent, can make the rate of profit whatever they like.

Second, the legal system of property which obtains in the capitalist world is out of line with economic reality. The capital gains which accrue to rentiers are the "reward" for no service.[17] Moreover, they introduce an inherently inflationary element into the economy. Finance which is spent upon investment creates incomes which can be spent over again for consumption.

Third, as the mixed-income class grows accustomed to placing their savings in equities (directly or through institutions such as investment trusts set up to accommodate them), an increasing amount of capital gains enter incomes with a relatively high propensity to consume, so that the overall ratio of saving to income is drifting down; the rate of profit corresponding to a given rate of growth therefore tends to rise as time goes by.

Of course, in the untranquil world there are many influences upon the Stock Exchange as a whole and on the valuation of particular firms as well as those that operate in the calm atmosphere of imagined steady growth. They are likely on the whole to contribute to instability, since expected profits cast a shadow

---

[17] Cf. J. K. Galbraith: "No grant of feudal privilege has ever equalled, for effortless return, that of the grandparent who bought and endowed his descendants with a thousand shares of General Motors or General Electric." *The New Industrial State*, p. 394.

before and tend to increase consumption out of profits just when investment is increasing.

In general, thriftiness plays a different role in this model from its role in Harrod's system. A high warranted rate of growth, due to a high value of *s,* tends to cause slumpy conditions and to inhibit growth. In our model, a higher propensity to save permits a higher level of real wages at a given rate of growth. It pushes back the "inflation barrier" at which real wages reach the tolerable minimum and so makes it possible for the firms to grow faster (if they are willing to do so); but firms serving the market for consumer goods do not like saving, which reduces their profits; they do all they can to keep it at bay with advertizement and innovations that generate psychological obsolescence, as well as by generating demand by turning unrealized needs into conscious desires.

INNOVATIONS

Technical progress was not easy to fit into the neoclassical concept of stationary equilibrium. Marshall's treatment of a growing economy with a constant normal rate of profit implies technical progress, and he evidently mixed acquired knowledge in with the conception of economies of scale (which take place with a growth of output but are not lost with a decline) [18] but the whole question was left very vague.

The Meaning of Neutral Inventions   Pigou discussed the effects of "inventions" in terms of a comparison of stationary equilibrium positions. He divided inventions into those which save labor, those which save "capital," and a wide neutral band in between which saves both. Hicks reduced neutrality to a point,

---

[18] *Principles*—Appendix H.

putting all improvements on one side or the other, into the labor-saving and the capital-saving categories. (This terminology, which is still widely used, is very confusing. All technical improvements, except those that merely save time,[19] increase output per head at some point in the process of production; in current discussions "labor-saving" is sometimes to be taken in the straightforward sense of reducing labor required for a given output and sometimes in the Hicksian sense of *more* labor-saving than neutral.)

The concept of a neutral invention is one that leaves the relative shares of wages and profits in proceeds the same in the new equilibrium position as in the old. Here there is an ambiguity; the technical nature of the change cannot determine the relative shares by itself, without reference to the capital to labor ratio in the new position. Hicks proposed, as the definition of neutrality, that the invention raises the marginal product of each "factor" equally when the "capital" per unit of labor is the same in the new position as the old. In what sense is "capital" to be taken? Let us suppose that we are comparing two equilibrium positions with the same labor employed, while in Alpha output per head is higher than in Beta as a result of superior technical knowledge, and let us suppose that the share of wages in the larger net output of Alpha is the same as in the smaller net output of Beta, that is, the relation between the two equilibria is neutral. Now suppose that the real-wage rate in Alpha is higher than in Beta in the same proportion as net output per head. Then, if the rate of profit is the same in the two positions, the value of capital per man is higher in Alpha in the same pro-

---

[19] For instance, a change of methods might be supposed to produce two crops a year, where there was formerly one, from the same land with the same amount of work. If each six-months crop is exactly half the former yearly crop, there is a saving of finance without any saving of factors of production.

portion as net output. If Hicks' constant "capital" per man is measured in labor time—that is, the value of capital divided by the real-wage rate—then the return per unit of capital in this sense has been raised in the same proportion as the wage rate; this satisfies the Hicks criterion of neutrality. If the argument is put into terms of the "one-commodity world" and capital is measured by a physical quantity of the commodity, then, if the real wage is higher in Alpha in the same proportion as net output per head, and commodity-capital per man is constant, the rate of profit is higher in the same proportion as the wage rate. But to have the same "capital" per man at a higher rate of profit implies a drastic fall in the propensity to save. On the other hand, if the propensity to save in Alpha is the same as in Beta, presumably the rate of profit is lower in Alpha (in a Pigovian stationary state). Then commodity-capital in Alpha must be higher than in Beta in a greater proportion than output. For relative shares to be constant, there must be a production function in Alpha (in terms of labor and the commodity as inputs with the commodity as output) of unit elasticity of substitution.

Harrod cut through these conundrums by proposing as the definition of neutrality a situation in which both the rate of profit and relative shares are unchanged. What was more important, he departed from the artificial concept of an invention as a shock moving equilibrium from one position to another; he conceived of technical progress going on continuously by a succession of innovations. Neutrality implies that innovations are scattered evenly throughout the economy so that output per head is raised at the same rate at all stages of the process of production; if we simplify the economy to two sectors, one producing commodities and one producing plant, then, when technical progress is neutral, and the rate of profit is constant, plant per man, measured in labor time, is constant and the value of capital per man is rising at the same rate as the real-wage rate.

(We can now describe a bias in technical progress, on either side of neutrality, as capital-using when, if the rate of profit were constant, the value of capital per man required by new technology would be rising faster than output per man; and as capital-saving in the contrary case.)

Harrod postulates a continuous, steady, and neutral rate of technical progress, given by God and the engineers, which raises output per head at a steady rate when the accumulation of capital is going on at a steady rate. The "natural" rate of growth is compounded of the rate of growth of the labor force and the rate of growth of output per head.[20] When the natural rate of growth is being realized, the capital to income ratio, the relative shares of wages and profits and the rate of profit are all constant through time.

There is something contradictory in postulating a uniform rate of profit throughout an economy in which technical progress is going on. Some firms are always taking advantage of new ideas faster than others and enjoying a higher rate of profit on their investments. Moreover, technical progress alters the nature of commodities and the requirements of skill and training of workers. However, there does not seem to be much hope of dealing with such problems until the main lines of a simplified analysis have been established. We therefore make the drastic assumptions that commodities and workers retain their physical characteristics and all technical change is concentrated in the design of equipment. Then output per head of consumer goods has an unambiguous meaning; on a steady growth path, the value of capital per man in terms of consumption goods is rising at the same rate as output per man and the capital to income ratio is constant. And we assume that the proportions of high-

---

[20] Sir Roy later introduced the idea of an *optimum* rate of growth, which is a much more complicated concept. See "Optimum Investment for Growth" in *Problems of Economic Dynamics: Essays in Honor of Michal Kalecki* (New York: Pergamon Press, 1966).

and low-profit investments remain constant through time, so that there is a constant overall rate of profit on capital. On this basis (though admittedly it is not very solid) we can apply the preceding argument in terms of *g, n,* and π to a growth path of steady with neutral technical progress.

The Vintage Model   When technical progress takes the form of designing improved equipment which reduces the labor and raw materials required per unit of output, we must suppose that each round of gross investment, say per year, goes into the newest and best equipment, while inferior equipment installed in the recent past is still in use.[21] The physical stock of capital equipment in existence at any moment depends upon the length of service life of plant, for this determines how many types, or vintages, of equipment, dating from earlier years, are in use at any moment alongside the latest and best which has just been installed. The longer the life of plant, the lower the output of labor equipped with the oldest plant and the lower the average output per head for the labor force as a whole. To avoid complications we confine the argument to the case of constant employment.

What determines the length of service life? To avoid some intricate points which add nothing of interest to the analysis, we may postulate that the potential physical lifetime of plant is longer than the service life, and that each plant has to be worked in exactly the same way over its life, neither gaining nor losing efficiency as time goes by. Its output therefore remains the same over its service life and the quasirent that it yields falls as the real-wage rate rises. (We shall continue to use the convention of constant prices of consumer goods, so that the rise in the real-

---

[21] See W. E. G. Salter, *Productivity and Technical Change* (Cambridge, 1960). Salter confines the theoretical part of his argument to perfect competition, which is an unnecessary restriction.

wages rate comes about through a rise in the money-wage rate.) On the steady growth path, the wage rate rises at the same rate as output per head. When a plant is first installed it has a higher quasirent than any older plant. Next year, its output is the same and its running costs have risen; the cost of materials, power, etc., bought from other firms is constant (like the prices of consumption goods) for rising wages offset increases in average output per head in producing them; the rise in prime costs for the plant is the rise in its own wage bill. (The interest cost of working capital has gone up correspondingly.) We may suppose that each plant is used until its quasirent has fallen to zero. It is then scrapped and the labor that was working it finds employment on the latest, most superior plant that is newly put into production.

In the simplest form of this argument, it is assumed that there are no prime costs except wages; then the plant is scrapped when its whole output is just less than sufficient to pay the wage bill.[22] In any case, prime costs (on our assumptions) rise each year with the rise in the wage bill. The time which it takes (at a given growth rate) to wipe out the quasirent of plant of any one vintage, depends upon the ratio of quasirent to wages of the latest and best plant. In short, the length of life of plant is a decreasing function of the share of wages in the value of net output. The share of wages depends upon the value of capital per man of a plant when new and on the rate of profit. To avoid overburdening the argument we may now return to the simple formula, $\pi = g/s_p$; and to postpone discussion of a point

---

[22] It has been argued that this concept is incompatible with imperfect competition (see D. Mario Nuti, "The Degree of Monopoly in the Kaldor-Mirrlees Growth Model," *Review of Economic Studies,* April 1969). However, part of wages go to quasi-overhead labor which would be required to keep the plant going at a minimum level of utilization so that prices still exceed short-period marginal cost even when quasirent has fallen to zero.

which we will take up later, we assume for the time being that the cost of capital per man embodied in a plant when new is independent of the rate of profit.[23] Then the share of wages varies only with the rate of profit. The higher the rate of profit, the greater the difference between the wage rate (at any moment) and the value of output per man with the latest equipment and therefore the longer the time which it will take to reduce its quasirent to zero (the growth rate being given) and the larger the number of vintages that will be in use at the date when it is scrapped. The greater the length of life of equipment, the lower the average output per man employed. At the same time, the proportion of the labor force that has to be re-equipped at each round is less when the life of plant is longer, so that the real resources required for gross investment are less.

By comparing paths exactly alike in all respects except for differences in the rate of profit, we can trace out another dimension of the pseudoproduction function. In terms of comparisons of Pigovian stationary states with different rates of profit, we traced out the vertical dimension of the pseudoproduction function, showing the choice of technique in a "given state of knowledge" and we saw that it may be so badly behaved as to contain backward-switch points, below which a technique with a higher output per head is associated with a higher rate of profit.[24] Along the horizontal dimension, showing the length of life of plant (at a given growth rate) the pseudoproduction function is

---

[23] There is only one superior technique invented at each round and labor-value prices of individual commodities and means of production rule as on Professor Samuelson's "surrogate" pseudoproduction function. (Cf. above, p. 36).

[24] See above, p. 61. For the time being we are assuming that the cost of plant when new is independent of the rate of profit. When this dimension of the pseudoproduction function is drawn with the share of wages in net output and the rate of profit as coordinates, a section of it conforming to our assumption is a straight line of which the slope represents the value of capital per man employed.

quite well behaved. A higher rate of output per head (with shorter life of equipment) is associated with a lower rate of profit. In a certain sense, it is associated with a higher ratio of capital to labor. There is no need to compare the stocks of capital in terms of value (which is a treacherous concept when the rate of profit is a variable); the point is that a shorter length of life entails a larger stock of capital in the sense that a higher rate of gross investment is required to maintain it. On any one path there is a constant proportion of the labor force occupied with investment and a constant stock of capital in terms of labor embodied, producing an output of commodities rising at the growth rate. As we move along the pseudoproduction function from a higher to a lower rate of profit, the proportion of the labor force in investment rises (for a larger amount of plant is being replaced every year). Thus the pseudoproduction function has the well-behaved characteristic of showing a higher capital to labor ratio (in the relevant sense) associated with a lower rate of profit.

Moreover, we can find here an analogy with the Wicksell process of "deepening" the stock of capital. A *rise* of output per head would be brought about by an *increase* in the share of gross investment in output, leading to a shorter length of life of plant. We must consider the significance of this for neoclassical theory.

Neoclassical Vintages　The model cannot work well in a pre-Keynesian setting, in which saving governs accumulation. In some versions,[25] it is taken for granted that the ratio of saving to net income (Harrod's s) is determined by the propensity to save out of household income. Then, at any moment, there is a

---

[25] See Ferguson, *op. cit.*, Chapters 13 and 14, for a comprehensive account of the vintage models that have been proposed by neo-neoclassical writers.

certain volume of saving per annum and there is a rate of interest at which firms are induced to carry out sufficient gross investment to produce net investment equal to this amount of saving. That rate of interest then determines the rate of profit, which influences the length of life of plant.[26] But this is not pre-Keynesian, it is bastard Keynesian. For Keynes, the influence of the rate of interest on the rate of investment (which in any case is rather a weak point in his system) [27] is produced by its relation to the expected rate of profit (or "marginal efficiency of capital"). To stimulate investment, the rate of interest (the cost of borrowing) has to be less than the expected rate of profit by a sufficient premium for risk, which, on a tranquil, steady growth path, must be assumed to be negligible. When the rate of profit is established, the banking system must be supposed to see to it that the rate of interest does not get out of line (otherwise equilibrium would be upset), but if there is nothing else in the story to determine the rate of profit, the rate of interest cannot do it.

Another argument consists in showing that, in a certain very special sense, the rate of return on investment to society as a whole is equal to the rate of profit. This is an ingenious use of the vintage model, which is worth repeating.

Taking all the assumptions of steady growth with perfect competition, let us postulate that there is a clear-cut division between the production of plant (which is the only capital good)

---

[26] In Professor Arrow's model, the propensity to save governs the share of *gross* investment in value of output. (This is finding an answer by changing the question.) The real-wage rate at any moment satisfies the condition of full employment. Then he is home. He set out to exhibit "learning by doing" but in fact he offers an ordinary vintage model in which technical progress is embodied in the design of equipment. The only difference is that the rate of progress is an increasing function of the amount of gross investment. See "The Economic Implications of Learning by Doing," *Review of Economic Studies* (June 1962).

[27] Cf. above, p. 83.

and the production, with the aid of plant, of commodities for consumption. Workers in the investment sector, with the aid of the equipment that they operate, maintain the stock of equipment that they need, at the same time as they produce plant for the consumption-good sector.

Now suppose that ten vintages of plant coexist in the consumption-good sector, each manned by a cohort of 100 teams of men. One plant employs one team throughout its life. There are no prime costs except the wage bill. Taking a year as the gestation period for plant, each vintage is used for ten years. At the end of that time the real wage has risen to absorb its whole output and it is scrapped. Now, when plant of vintage V_{10} is being constructed, the households, by consuming less than usual, release resources to have 101, instead of the usual 100, plants built. Thereafter investment returns to 100 plants a year. To man the extra plant, a team must be taken from vintage V_1 which is entering its last year of life. Next year only 99 teams are released when the remaining V_1 plants are scrapped. A team has to be taken from V_2 to man the hundredth V_{11} plant, one from V_3 to man the hundredth V_{12} plant, and so on until V_{10} enters the last year of its life. One team is then transferred to V_{19}. At the end of the year the remaining 100 teams are released and go to V_{20}. The normal position is then restored.

Now, the additional output, over and above what would have been available without the extra V_{10} plant, in the first year consists of the output of one V_{10} team minus the output of one V_1 team. The V_1 output was scarcely more than the real wage of a team at the rate then ruling. Thus the additional output this year is approximately equal to the quasirent on a V_{10} plant in the first year of its life. Next year the additional output is the output of a V_{10} team minus the output of a V_2 team, which is approximately this year's wage. Over the ten years, it is thus equal to the series of quasirents of a plant, which yields the normal rate of profit on its initial cost. Thus (assuming that the economy was flexible enough to permit one extra plant to be built without additional cost) the extra consumption is equal to the rate of profit on the extra investment.[28]

This shows that when the economy is growing in equilibrium with any given rate of profit, the rate of return, in this peculiar sense, is equal to that rate of profit.

Another favorite argument is to point out that the wage rate is equal to the marginal product of labor. At any moment, a small reduction in the labor force would mean that some of the oldest plant (just about to be scrapped) would cease to be used. When the wage bill is the only element in prime cost and there is perfect competition, the reduction in output (the marginal product) is equal to the reduction in the wage bill. Similarly, a small increase in the labor force could be accommodated by postponing the scrapping of some of the oldest plant (but it would need a rise in the level of effective demand to make it worthwhile to do so). There is of course no sense in which the marginal product determines the wage; the age of the oldest plant, therefore its output, and the wage rate are determined together by technical conditions and the rate of profit.

Lacking a theory of distribution, the only resort for a neo-classical vintage model is to treat the economy as though it were managed by the committee of a kibbutz.[29] (We continue to assume that a constant amount of work is always being done, though this is not here very reasonable.) If the committee has decided upon the proportion of the labor force to be occupied in producing plant (taking the conditions of our last example) and the stock of equipment (in both sectors) has been built up accordingly, the cooperative will be following exactly the same

[28] The above passage is taken (with minor alterations) from a review of Professor Solow's *Capital Theory and the Rate of Return*. See Joan Robinson, *Collected Economic Papers* (Oxford: Blackwell, 1965), vol. 3.
[29] Cf. above, p. 33.

136 / *Economic Heresies*

path as would be followed by an economy in which the rate of profit was such as to be associated with the same allocation of resources between the sectors. As each new plant in the consumption-good sector becomes available, labor to man it is taken from the least productive plant still in use, thus establishing the same length of life as would occur where incomes consisted of profits and wages, though the distribution of consumption goods among the members of the cooperative may be on any principles that they find acceptable. (They might use a notional wage rate for accounting purposes, though in the simplified conditions of our example it would not be necessary—calculations in real terms would be adequate to their requirements.)

But what determines the proportion of labor allocated to investment? Here the neo-neoclassical theorem or golden rule comes into the argument.[30] Up to a certain point, an increase in the permanent allocation of labor to the investment sector leads on to a path (when equilibrium in the length of life of plant has been established) on which consumption is higher at each phase of technical progress than it would have been on the former path. The limit to this process of "deepening" the stock of capital is reached when the life of plant has been reduced to such a length that to move one more team of workers over to the investment sector would add to future output (by shortening the length of life of plant) no more than would be lost by taking them away from the consumption-good sector. At this point there is nothing to be gained from a further rise in the ratio of the stock of capital measured in labor time to labor currently employed.

The committee of the cooperative might work this out directly

---

[30] See Joan Robinson, *Essays in the Theory of Economic Growth*, p. 136 (London: Macmillan, 1963).

or they might find the notional rate of profit, at any point, corresponding to a notional wage rate equal to the output per head of the oldest plant and compare it to the rate of growth. The rate of growth is the technological rate of discount or objective "cost of waiting" for the economy; [31] so long as the notional rate of profit is greater than this, there is a possibility of gaining consumption in the future (above what it would otherwise be) by raising the share of investment in output. The committee might consider it right to aim for the maximum or they might bring a subjective rate of discount of the future into their calculations and aim to stop short, with a somewhat longer length of life of plant (and smaller share of investment).

When they have decided upon the objective that they propose to aim at, they have to consider the pace at which they should go toward it. The most heroic course would be to put all the labor becoming available into the investment sector as soon as a certain tolerable minimum level of consumption has been achieved. This would reach the objective in the shortest possible time, but it would be extravagant. Investment is accelerating as men are released (by the rise in output per head) from producing the constant supply of consumption goods. Part of the labor in the investment sector has to be occupied with increasing its own stock of equipment. It might be technically impossible to tailor the stock of investment-sector equipment so that none of it became redundant at the moment when investment settled down to its permanent level. A less drastic course would be to

---

[31] The rate of growth (which is exogenously given by technical progress) is the rate of return from the point of view of society on a unit of gross investment embodied in improved technique. The notional profit includes the surplus of consumption over the notional wage bill. When the notional rate of profit has been reduced to equality with the rate of growth and all consumption is included in the notional wage bill there is no further gain in future consumption to be had by reducing present consumption.

work the proportion of labor in the investment sector up to the level that will be permanently required and then to accumulate plant, at the pace which this provides, until a stock with the required age-composition has been built up, consumption being allowed to increase meanwhile. Or a longer period of adjustment might be allowed with a higher level of consumption in the earlier stages and a smaller acceleration. (The neoclassicals claim to be able to advise the committee on the ideal program, taking into account the rate of fall of the marginal utility of consumption goods as consumption per head rises. Or, examining the program that has been decided upon, they deduce the implicit time-pattern required to justify it.)

Our story of the kibbutz would not throw much light on the problems facing the authorities in charge of a national investment plan. We have to set it out only to illustrate the application to the problem of accumulation of the neoclassical philosophy of social harmony, separating it from the problems of the distribution of income between wages and profits.

The maximum stock of capital that the cooperative could aim to achieve, given by the golden rule, is that which is appropriate to a rate of profit equal to the rate of growth. This rate of profit obtains when all wages are consumed and all profits saved. Here is a meeting point between the neo-neoclassics and their critics, though the former do not usually emphasize the inference that consumption of unearned income is deleterious to society.[32]

---

[32] Here $s_p = 1$, $s_w = 0$. Suppose that $s_p = 1$ and there is also some saving out of wages ($s_w > 0$). Then π is less than g. Capitalists have not enough profits to finance investment and they borrow from workers. The length of life of plant appropriate to this rate of profit is so short as to *reduce* consumption at any point on the path below the maximum because of the excessive amount of labor in the investment sector.

INDUCED BIAS

We must now open the gate impounding the assumption that the cost of plant when new is independent of the rate of profit. When only one superior technique is invented at each round, the physical specification of plant and the labor embodied in it are independent of prices; comparing two paths with different rates of profit, the value of capital per man may be higher or lower, where the rate of profit is lower. When the two rates of profit are at separate points on the same pseudoproduction function, the design of plant is also different. When the two points lie on either side of a forward-switch point, the lower rate of profit is associated with a higher value of capital. This means that the share of wages tends to be lower, which tends to make the length of life of plant longer. A longer life of plant entails a lower overall value of the stock of capital corresponding to a given value of plant when new. Thus the more well behaved the pseudoproduction function is in the vertical dimension, the less so it is in the horizontal dimension. When the two techniques are divided by a backward-switch point, the lower rate of profit is associated with a lower value of capital, so that (for a given rate of growth) the life of plant is all the shorter.

But what is all this about? How can a single pseudoproduction function be continually re-created as technical progress goes on? On each path, a succession of new superior techniques are being invented year by year. How can there be any systematic relation between separate series, each appropriate to a different path? One pseudoproduction function for a number of Pigovian stationary states is already an artificial construction; to postulate a succession of them, all of identical shape, moving at a steady pace through time, is merely absurd.

Indeed, as soon as we introduce technical progress into the story, a "natural" rate of growth, exogenously given, is an unnatural concept. The engineers who design plant are employed, directly or indirectly, by the firms who are going to install it; prospects of profit influence design. Moreover, actual accumulation does not proceed smoothly. The kind of innovations called for when there is a high rate of investment going on and labor is hard to recruit are not the same as those induced by pressure to cut costs in a depression. And over the long run, history and geography shape the path that each economy follows. Where prospects of profit are high, finance is easy to come by; where labor is scarce, capital-using innovations are favored; where there is a plentiful reserve of labor in an overpopulated countryside, capital-saving innovations make rapid development possible. However capital is measured, the capital to labor ratio is higher in the United States than in Japan, but they are not two points on the same production function.[33]

There is another aspect of technology which is of far greater importance than its profitability. After fifty years, Pigou's emphasis on the difference between the real cost to society of producing saleable goods and the money cost to profit-seeking firms is beginning to be appreciated. The nature of technology depends very much upon what the public can be induced to put up with.

---

[33] Cf. above, p. 106.

CONCLUSION

It is easy enough to make models on stated assumptions. The difficulty is to find the assumptions that are relevant to reality. The art is to set up a scheme that simplifies the problem so as to make it manageable without eliminating the essential character of the actual situation on which it is intended to throw light. Keynes found out that the doctrines still orthodox in the interwar period were drawn from models which require the assumption that the wage bargain is made in terms of the employer's product and that the decisions of households to save govern the rate of investment that firms undertake. These assumptions have been smuggled back into neo-neoclassical models. All the pother about the meaning of "capital" has been subsidiary to this. The special assumptions of a "one-commodity world" are required for a model in which the real-wage rate tends to the level that assures full employment.[1] The further assumptions of

---

[1] Cf. above, p. 69. In the one-commodity model, both the pre-Keynesian assumptions are fulfilled together. In a two-sector model of the neo-neoclassical type, "capital" has all the same characteristics as in the one-commodity case, while the consumption good is made of a different physical substance. There is then a price of one in terms of the other, which varies with the division of net output between the two. The second pre-Keynesian assumption is brought in to determine this division. The assumptions are conscientiously explained by Professor Meade in *A Neoclassical Theory of Growth* (London: Allen & Unwin, 1961).

141

perfect competition and the instantaneous establishment of equilibrium are then added in order to be able to demonstrate that the real wage is equal to the marginal product of labor.

It has often been suggested that this scheme of thought is the result of ideological bias, but it is unnecessary to raise that question unless the models can pass the test of consistency and relevance. In the foregoing essays, a serious objection has been raised to their logical structure on account of their treatment of time: they seem to be unable to distinguish between coexisting differences and sequential change. Even if they could pass the test of consistency, they would fail on relevance. They are, as Professor Solow says, "cheap vehicles"; [2] in fact they are too rickety to stir from the spot where they stand—as soon as any one of their peculiar assumptions is relaxed the model collapses and we have to start all over again on our own feet.

We can surely agree to start again where Keynes left off. Who wants to deny that the future is uncertain; that investment decisions, in a private-enterprise economy, are made by firms rather than by households; that wage rates are offered in terms of money, or that prices of manufactures are not formed by the higgling of a perfectly competitive market?

A model that is intended to be relevant to some actual problem must take account of the mode of operation of the economy to which it refers. "Pure theorists" sometimes take a supercilious attitude to "structuralists" or "institutionalists." They prefer a theory that is so pure as to be uncontaminated with any material content. Was Keynes an institutionalist? He took into account the institutions of a nation-state, of the organization of industry, the banking system and the Stock Exchange as he saw them. Since his day, there have been important changes in the setting

---

[2] See "On the Rate of Return: Reply to Pasinetti," *Economic Journal* (June 1970).

in which theory has to operate. Partly as the result of the change in ideology associated with his name, the governments of capitalist industrialized nations play an enormously greater part in the management of their economies than formerly. Each hopes to adopt policies that will maintain near-full employment (which implies a high level of profits) and continuous growth for its own economy, while avoiding excessive inflation, maintaining a positive balance of trade on income account and equilibrium in its balance of payments. The policies that each adopts react upon the others. The greater internal coherence of national policies makes international anarchy all the worse. Meanwhile, the growth of the huge national and international corporations is establishing independent seats of power which cut across or manipulate the policies of national governments.

There are signs that the 1970s may prove to be the testing time for modern capitalism. Is it possible to maintain near-full employment without undue inflation? Can an international monetary system be devised that will stand up to strains that national policies put upon it? Even if the crises that are looming up are overcome and a new run of prosperity lies ahead, deeper problems will still remain. Modern capitalism has no purpose except to keep the show going. To prevent severe unemployment and to keep real wages rising secures the adherence of the workers, growing consumption keeps the public in general complacent, and opportunities for profit encourage industry to expand.

National economic success is identified with statistical GNP. No questions are asked about the content of production. The success of modern capitalism for the last twenty-five years has been closely bound up with the armaments race and the trade in weapons (not to mention wars when they are used); it has not succeeded in overcoming poverty in its own countries, and has not succeeded in helping (to say the least) to promote development in the Third World. Now we are told that it is in the course of making the planet uninhabitable even in peacetime.

It should be the duty of economists to do their best to enlighten the public about the economic aspects of these menacing problems. They are impeded by a theoretical scheme which (with whatever reservations and exceptions) represents the capitalist world as a kibbutz operated in a perfectly enlightened manner to maximize the welfare of all its members.

INDEX